Cont

Author's Note

All these articles, in somewhat different form, originally appeared in *The New Yorker*, with the exception of the one called 'Bangs, Roars, Shrieks and Sighs', which was published in *Contact*. I am indebted to the editors of these magazines for permission to republish here.

Alan Moorehead

The Villa Diana

Chapter One

A Street Car
Named Boccaccio

The Villa Medici stands high up on Fiesole above Florence and the valley of the Arno, looking pretty much the same to-day as it did when Michelozzo built it in 1458 and Lorenzo the Magnificent is supposed to have given his literary dinner parties there towards the end of the century. The Villa Diana lies a little further down the hill at the end of an old Etruscan road that winds among olive groves and lines of cypresses: and this was the house where a certain Agnolo Ambrogini, better known as Poliziano, moved in about 1483 so that he should be conveniently placed, both for accepting invitations to the literary dinners and for educating Lorenzo's three children.

During the battle for Florence in the last war the Villa Medici was pock-marked by shellfire here and there and the property stands empty now. The Villa Diana was occupied at different times by the troops of seven different armies, but otherwise escaped damage, if one overlooks the looting of the grand piano and the linen. I leased it from the present owner, a man who now lives in California, in September, 1948, and have been living here ever since.

It has been an experience that probably serves as well as anything else to illustrate a certain type of life in Europe now – that indigestible mixture of feudal habits, Marxian politics, religion and the new dollar economy that flows round any place with a history and a name. We live, of course, in surroundings of extreme physical beauty and that no doubt has an influence – though whether towards violence or the quietening of the nerves I have not yet been able to find out.

The day we arrived Paola, the cook, was standing on the front steps smiling and waving between two sixteenth-century stone lions, and the ancient façade of the villa rose up behind her with that suggestion of enormity which I used to have as a small boy looking up at a city bank. I asked her who did all the work round the place.

'I do,' Paola said. She picked up two trunks and then trotted in front of us through the house throwing open windows and shutters.

Apart from a network of cellars and the chapel there were 17 rooms in all, which is not very big the way Florentine villas go. There was no telephone, no frigidaire, no gas, no electrical power other than for lighting. Paola cooked on charcoal and the kitchen was immense.

'You will have to get someone to help you,' we said. And that was the beginning of something which I can only describe as a mass movement of population. Maria, the 'daily', appeared, then Santina the housemaid, together with her four-year-old daughter Anna Grazia, then Battista, a gardener of terrifying aspect aged seventy or a hundred, then Paola's husband, Annunzio (a dyer who went to dye in Florence every morning but who was willing to place the rest of his time at my disposal) and Luigi, Paola's schoolboy son.

The second week brought to light the Contadino who worked the farm around the house, an indeterminate and rather pathetic little figure known as the Contadino's Boy, who brought the milk every morning, and Signora Bianca, the sitter-cum-governess. Besides these a host of tradesmen, tradesmen's children, friends, relations and chance acquaintances. There was the olive-presser, the wine-dealer, the agent, the curtain-hanger, and an itinerant barber who walked down from Fiesole with his scissors in his hand.

I am apt to go into the kitchen now and find a sizeable group of strangers who rise and bow with considerable warmth and amiability. Unidentified children accompanied by dogs pass through the front hall and occasionally nod. Once a water-diviner called briefly and I recall being introduced in the pantry to a Professor Zucci who was selling bees.

'My God,' my wife said, 'there must be an end to it somewhere.'

There is, however, no end in Italy. No man here, in the sense that John Donne and Mr Hemingway intended, is an island. We are all very much part of the Main and the servants are hopelessly involved in the full range of our intrigues, amours and tragedies; and we in theirs. When the church bell tolls just a few yards up the hill behind the house it tolls for every man jack of us: it means, possibly, that one of the seasonal processions to bless the crops or commemorate the Saints is about to come winding down through the olive trees. The small man carrying the Cross on a stout leather belt slung round his shoulders will be Annunzio, and the choir boy singing up in front will be the Contadino's Boy, miraculously transformed into a Della Robbia cherub with clean hands and a spotless white surplice. Possibly it's a marriage. On these days I always receive a formal request for permission for the procession to pass through my garden, and this is accompanied by the gift of a little white box, bound up with flowers and cellophane, containing two iced almonds and a card from the bride and bridegroom. We die, marry and get born here with astonishing frequency, and every time something happens the bell tolls. It's one of the oldest inhabited parts of Italy or Europe, and for a district that has been given up to a fairly steady routine of murder, rapine and savagery for the last two thousand years, there is an unusually hopeful expectation of life among the people. Paola's parents are 85. There was surprise and dismay last year when one of Annunzio's aunts, aged 95, complained that she was not feeling well.

Most of life through these long years is given up to work. It starts in the Villa Diana around half past five or six in the morning when Annunzio fans the charcoal into a blaze and Santina pulls down the iron bars from the doors and windows; (nothing much has been stolen yet but we have a burglar complex here). It goes on through the morning in a cascade of arguments and gossip until after lunch, when it stops for an hour or two and most of us go to bed. From four onwards it continues again intermittently until midnight. This happens on seven days a week except on saint's days and *festas*. Sunday is the day when between intervals at church the young men take their double-barrelled shotguns into the lovely countryside and blow the living daylights out of the thrushes and the bullfinches which they sell in the market on Monday morning.

Quite a number of the older people can neither read or write. They live in unheated cottages without sewerage or running water and often an entire family – anything up to six or seven – will sleep in the same bed. Santina, the housemaid, aged 26, had never been to a theatre before she took a day off last week, and when at Christmas she set off to visit her parents in the mountains we found that she had no coat. Her parents live in a village which can only be reached after a ten mile walk through the snow. In the hills diet consists of brown bread, fruit, vegetables, pasta, wine and oil; in the morning a cauldron is put on to boil and into it are dropped the vegetables in season and perhaps a little pasta. This is their breakfast, lunch and dinner, their coffee, roast and pudding all rolled into one. On fête days they might have a sweet cake, possibly a little veal. They know nothing of dentists, telephones, automobiles, nylon, deep freeze or Mr Frank Sinatra.

All around them, in the great palaces of Florence and the ancient churches and villas on the surrounding hills, is perhaps the greatest heritage of the human intellect ever gathered together into a single place: among the artists, sculptors and architects who worked here there are such names as Michelangelo, Botticelli, Donatello, Leonardo da Vinci, Piero della Francesca and Giotto; among the poets, Dante, among the lawgivers, Machiavelli and Lorenzo, among the orators Savonarola, and apart from these there is a large group of less brilliant all-rounders like Cellini who seemed to be able to do anything from designing a silver salt cellar or writing a classic to building fortifications for the city. In Florence at this moment there is a street-car named Boccaccio.

Probably there is more learning here to the square mile, more museums, libraries, art galleries, more skilled craftsmanship, especially in such things as embroidered silks and leather, than in any other city of half a million inhabitants in the world. Even at the dead winter season

A Street Car Named Boccaccio

the shops are full of hams, cheeses, fruit, meats and hard liquor such as you would hardly see in California or Fifth Avenue. But the people can't buy these expensive things, they don't go into the museums. They sit in the back streets and in the frosty villages eating minestrone and working. And, to the outward eye, they appear to be more cheerful, better-mannered, and more agreeable to live with than any other people in Europe. Psychoanalysts are almost unknown.

If there is a secret behind all this, and there probably is, it has not yet been revealed by the large numbers of writers and foreign tourists who have been hurrying through Italy since the end of the war. Most of them pause to remark that the country is bursting with high spirits but bedevilled with the most appalling poverty – and they leave the matter hanging there in the air without an answer. It is when you live here, even as a foreigner who only sees a small part of the game and this probably from a prejudiced angle, that you find yourself every day surrounded by a whole variety of answers, a regular barrage of explanations which, like the weather-cock nature of the Italian mind itself, alters with every wind that blows and the season of the year.

There's the medical approach: according to this it's all bound up with the oil the Italians use for cooking, the wine and spaghetti they consume and the sunshine. There's the political line (non-Marxist department) which explains that the Italians never did believe in central government – they are just natural anarchists and that's the way we would all be if we were left to ourselves. Then you have the religious theory that these people, almost alone in the midst of the cynicism of the West and the false materialist fervour of the Russians, have a faith in which they really believe and this carries them through life with a basic sense of peace; and the puritan theory that only through work can man be happy – and certainly the Italians work.

Finally there is the philosophic explanation (rather hazy this one, and strictly conservative) which affirms that most of the inventions of the twentieth century – the telephone, radio, motor-cycles, aeroplanes, atomic bombs, electric razors and deep-freeze – have brought us nothing but misery; and since most Italians are far too poor to have the benefit of these things they live the simple down-to-earth life and are consequently much happier.

Maybe there is some truth in all these points but it's hard to put your finger on it and say just which point has the most validity on any particular day. In the Villa Diana I find we coast along in a fairly equitable fashion for ten days or so – nothing worse happens than two of the chickens are stolen (despite the fact that Annunzio has an elaborate system of ropes and pulleys connecting the door of the hen run to the foot of his bed), a mouse has got into the wine or a bee stings the Contadino's Boy; then suddenly *presto* we are in the midst of the most hellish tragedy. A wild ululation comes up from the kitchen and Santina is discovered in tears. Her baby Anna Grazia is freezing to death at the convent. She knows it. She feels it. The child is being maltreated.

We all know about Anna Grazia and feel deeply. When the seven separate armies swept through here in the course of the war they left behind them many an Anna Grazia, carelessly, as soldiers will. It was represented to me when Santina was first brought to the Villa Diana that it was a patriotic duty for me to employ her since her child was the offspring of an English soldier, a sergeant, it was said, from somewhere in Yorkshire, though Santina could not recall his name. This I frankly disbelieved until Anna Grazia herself was produced, smiling happily up at us through the palest blue eyes. She had a halo of fine hair and two large red ears that were the very breath of Yorkshire.

Anna Grazia was parked out in a nearby convent and all went well through the long warm fall days. But now the Tramontana has begun to blow and we have Santina in tears.

'All right Santina,' my wife says, 'you can bring her here to live with us as long as the cold weather lasts.'

More tears and then another outburst. It seems now that Santina has been up all night with a poisoned finger. It does indeed look very bad, though not perhaps so bad that, as Santina herself suggests, she is about to die. She rejects with a piercing scream any idea of calling a doctor. 'Signora! Signora!' she wails, 'he'll cut me up.' Our doctor in fact is an exceptionally mild little man usually to be seen chugging round the streets of Florence on a one-stroke motor bicycle, and famous for never sending in a bill. As he advances into the house Santina shrinks fainting into the linen cupboard with wild Hogarthian thoughts of butcher's knives and two-handed saws revolving through her mind. We pin her down at last long enough for the doctor to examine her hand and remark that a hot compress ought to do the job.

And this is the moment when a crash from the kitchen announces that the cat has got the Sunday joint, together with four fine old bowls of Venetian glass; and the postman is at the door with a telegram which says that Annunzio's aunt has succumbed during the night. The funeral will be at four in the afternoon.

These scenes – and they are often a good deal more complicated than this – are apt to strain the nerves at the time; but normally all is peace and happiness again on the following day. Provided you can get used to the sensation of constantly skating on thin ice – the feeling that every hour may suddenly project you into Elysian fields or down into the utmost pit of hell – then it's not a bad existence, and certainly you have the sensation of living life as it really is, without affectation or boredom. The key to it all seems to be that you let the tragedy or the joy come out, immediately, as soon as it hits you, and the more people to share it with the better. This is no field in which the psychoanalyst can work.

We employed one girl who had a story as painful as any, and in a way very expressive of Italy just now. She was married before the war and had a child. Then her husband went off to fight. It seems hard to believe it now but there was a time when Mussolini was taking on Russia as well as America and the British. He sent several divisions to help the Germans in the Ukraine and this girl's husband was one of the officers. Since then – nothing. She doesn't know whether he is dead or alive because she has never had a single letter nor any address to which she could write. The chances are that he is one of the millions the Russians captured and sent, like so many animals, to Siberia and the east. A number of Italians (incidentally the Russians' allies for the last two years of the war), are reputed to be in the salt mines and he may be one of these.

But now it's eight years since this boy went away, and the point for his wife is – is she married or not? More complicated still – if he did come back would he not be a complete stranger ? During these seven years she has been waiting, getting along on a pension of eight dollars a month and what the relatives can spare. Because she is in love with him she has remained faithful, even though the church now says that she may marry again.

I was commiserating with her one day when she said softly: 'I suppose it isn't too bad. You see, we weren't getting along very well before he left. We had only been married two years but he had another girl.'

So you can't then very easily get to the end of anything in Italy. Where, in a country like Italy, do the loyalties lie? At one moment they are fighting the Americans and British, and the next they are on their side. Within a decade they have been asked to support first a dictator, then a king, then a republic. One has a certain sympathy with a fascist, a good friend of the late Count Ciano, who was exclaiming here the other day: 'What were Mussolini and the Fascist Party for if not to fight Russian communism? We were the pioneers. What did we get for our trouble? We were defeated in the war; I personally was put on trial for my life and imprisoned. And now the Americans come along and tell me to go right back to where I was and start hating the Russians again.'

It is this complication of communism with fascism which is the interesting thing, especially in a place like Florence. This city, a great playground of the Anglo-American rich in the lush years between the two wars, seems to prove again a strange rule that is fairly general in Europe now – wherever you get a place that has been famous for its beauty and the luxury of its tourist trade there now you will find the communists particularly entrenched. Maybe it's because the tourist trade has fallen off so much, leaving so many people unemployed, but whatever the reason we have in Florence one of the red strongholds of Italy. It is communism on three different levels, very difficult to disentangle. Technically the rank and file are pure Marxists – redistribution of property, nationalisation of the banks and so forth – but with one or two little additions: they would not perhaps discard the Roman Catholic Church entirely any more than they would really reject Marshall Aid, and they are certainly prepared to get tough with people like the Jugoslavs over such questions as Trieste. In other words, National Communism, which may bear some resemblance to Fascism.

Then there is the smaller and more select group which follows the way of the Comintern. They are prepared to spread the word internationally, they accept the present party line as untouchable dogma because this is a time of crisis and they argue that a return to liberal Leninism can be made later on when we are all comfortably settled under the red flag.

Finally there are those – very few, very select – who are just simply Russian and treat the whole mess as a field for the exercise of the old power politics: Russia *versus* the Rest. These agents are much more concerned with meeting the big Italian industrialists and politicians than the rank and file.

Togliatti, the leader of the party, is widely believed to be a purist, a kind of Italian Tito, and, therefore, not particularly well regarded in Moscow. He would let communism develop in its own way in Italy and skip the dogma for the moment.

Is it for this reason that most people here think that Russia for some time past has been holding back the communists in Italy? The last thing that Russia wants, they argue, is to be forced to go to war on behalf of a communist party which is firstly Marxist and Italian and only secondly Russian. Same thing with France. Russia, according to this argument, might be willing to keep both Italy and France in a ferment by subsiding the communists here – but war, no, neither civil nor international. Not until the east is settled and a few awkward problems like Tito are composed. Thus Russia made no attempt to intervene in the Italian general elections in 1948 and there have been very few signs of direct interference since then.

It is an interesting theory if only for the fact that it leads one on to the pleasant conclusion that war won't come for a year or two at any rate.

In Florence, as in most other parts of Italy, the membership of the party has been falling off since the last elections (when they counted on one-third of the vote), but the more thoughtful of the right wing politicians here do not take much account of this. They point out that there are always a large number of waverers who drop off in the slack periods, and the communists will no doubt scoop them up again as we approach another crisis. At the moment nobody else seems to be bothering greatly about them. Prices are rising steadily, much more rapidly than wages, and unemployment continues just about where it was a year ago: about two million.

I know an able young Italian in Florence who speaks perfect English and has a college education. When he was a prisoner of war in South Africa they let him out on parole and he earned eight dollars a day. Then he was repatriated to Italy and for 18 months on his return he never so much as even heard of a job. The result is, like millions of others here, he doesn't really have much faith in the regeneration of Italy through communism or anything else. He thinks it's too crowded, too complicated by ancient custom and he wants to get away – preferably to the USA. The ordinary city worker and his family have a vision of countries like America that is not much short of heaven: automobiles for everyone, lots of money, plenty of jobs, splendid apartments, television. This is largely the result of the impact of the American movies and perhaps the occasional appearance of an American tourist going by in a large car, spending a month's wage on a single dinner. A kind of fairy-tale glow has settled over all things American; given a chance the unemployed Italian would probably elect to be an American first and a communist second. Thus he is often a communist by default. His reason might yearn towards Marx but the flesh is weak and he hungers for the United States.

You will find the most devout Party members thronging into the latest Hollywood movie, which is full of sinister capitalistic values, and he will ignore the most simple and excellent Italian film (*I Ladri di Biciclette* for example) which is being shown a little further down the street. He wants to be entertained; he doesn't want to see a faithful representation of his own life. His attitude in fact reflects that of the trecento primitive painters in Siena, who practically ignored such matters as landscape, perspective and natural grouping but concentrated instead on making an artificial pattern. Presumably they argued: 'If you want to see real people and real landscape go outside and look at them for yourself.'

Admittedly this is something you can do in Tuscany and never grow tired. Even in January we have days of icy sunshine and nothing but a sky of heavy Prussian blue arching overhead It is especially along the road from Florence to Siena, probably the most civilised landscape offering anywhere. Each hilltop has its sprawling pink farmhouse and a line of marching cypresses. Each hillside has its patchwork of vines and olives. Each bend of the road an avenue of trees, haphazardly spaced beside a crumbling wall. Nothing is emphatic, nothing precisely in or out of place; nothing less ancient than a thousand years. The countryside glides away before you, endlessly and faultlessly repeating itself with the persistence of a green pattern on a green carpet. Even the villages seem to be dotted about with the inevitability – the change in sameness – of a well-set dinner table.

Usually, at every other corner of the road, a team of white oxen stands up, mild and enormous; these are the huge Chiana breed, not much smaller than elephants. Little red tassels dangle between the four foot span of their horns to keep the flies off their angelic faces. The Italian businessmen returning from their weekend villas tear by at a hundred kilometres an hour to catch the opening of the bourse in Milan.

In Florence the market goes a good deal slower. Twice a week the farmers and the buyers gather in the Piazza Signoria under the shadow of the Uffizi Gallery and Michelangelo's *David*. They produce little bottles of wine and oil for sampling, and pocketfuls of grain which they cascade down from the right hand to the left like a conjurer with a deck of cards. When a deal is made, buyer and seller grip hands and shake three times emphatically. Then the witness steps between them and, with a smart chop of his arm breaks them apart. This is as good as a signed contract, even enforceable in law. No man, except in extraordinary circumstances, would break such an agreement and go back to that market again.

Except for a few spots along the river there is not much sign of war damage in Florence now. The big issue of course is the question of the bridges. The Germans in their retreat blew up five of them, including the Ponte Santa Trinita which many people believe was the most beautiful bridge in the world. They left the more famous Ponte Vecchio intact but destroyed a few acres of ancient buildings at either end of it to block the approaches. It now seems from new evidence that has turned up that none of this would have happened but for a series of odd and very hysterical incidents in the summer of 1944.

The Germans apparently wanted to make Florence an open city (Hitler had been down here twice and in a glow of artistic conscience had given express orders about it); but Kesselring and the German command were furious with the Allies over what had happened at Rome. They claimed that the Allies had expressly agreed that if Rome were declared an open city, and the bridges across the Tiber left standing, then the British and American soldiers would go

The Sienna Road

round the city and not through it. However the Allies did march through Rome and thereby succeeded in grabbing a part of Kesselring's rearguard; and he was determined that this was not going to happen again in Florence. An attempt was made through the Vatican to contact Field Marshal Alexander, the Allied Commander-in-Chief, but no answer was received. Despite this (so the German story runs) orders were given to leave the bridges intact.

Then three things happened. The Allies raided and partly destroyed Dresden (which the Germans regarded as their Florence), the attempt was made on Hitler's life; and finally Allied aircraft flew over Florence dropping leaflets addressed to the Italian residents and signed by Field Marshal Alexander. These pamphlets urged the Italians to sabotage any attempt made by the Germans to blow up the bridges; and this last incident seems to have maddened a certain Colonel Fuchs, who was commanding a rearguard of paratroopers in Florence. He ordered all the bridges to be mined at once and evacuated the Italian civilians from along the river bank. An exception was made of the Ponte Vecchio, partly because Hitler, back in Germany, was still fussing about it, and partly because there was a superstructure of three-storey buildings running across it – the famous gallery that connects the Uffizi to the Pitti Palace. The Arno was very low at this time of the year and it was seen that the debris of these buildings would simply make a convenient causeway for the Allies across the stream.

The bridges went up with a terrific bang and Santa Trinita with its four lovely statues representing the seasons of the year vanished from human sight after nearly four hundred years of service. Lately workmen have been dredging in the river and they have hauled up quite a number of the original stones including the four statues, all of them in pretty good shape, with the exception of Spring who has lost her head. With money largely subscribed from the United States an exact replica of Santa Trinita is now to be built.

Incidentally people here have been made all the more eager about the Santa Trinita since it was discovered during the war that it was designed from some original drawings of Michelangelo.

The other story which has moved Florence deeply is the affair of the three huge doors on the Baptistery in front of the cathedral, executed by Ghiberti and Pisano. Michelangelo himself referred to them as worthy to be the gates of paradise, and much later on tourists like Alexandre Dumas were writing about 'this marvellous bronze.' Ghiberti alone spent fifty years working on his two doors, and for some centuries it has been agreed that they are among the very best things that Italy has.

Midway through the war the Italians took them down and stored them in a disused railway tunnel south of Florence. When the front line began to move up Italy the Germans produced a special train and got the doors back into Florence again for greater safety (and in fact the railway tunnel was bombed soon afterwards). In 1946 it was decided that the doors should have a polish before being put back into the Baptistery again; and this was the moment when one of the workmen discovered he was polishing, not bronze, but gold. All three doors were then found to be thickly encrusted with it.

This is the kind of pleasant surprise that extends back through centuries. For some four hundred years everyone had referred to the 'bronze doors'; the surface looked like bronze and it felt like bronze. What had happened was that the city dust of many generations had collected on the doors and most people had forgotten about the gold. All three doors were put back in their places in 1948 and they look pretty fine, especially when the sunshine slants down across the cathedral and joins its colour to the gold. Usually you will find a group of Florentines and tourists hanging round them.

Inspired by this there is a good deal of cleaning of fifteenth-century masterpieces going on in Florence just now, and by the time the tourist rush sets in again with the spring, several other re-discoveries will be on show. Nearly all the Uffizi paintings (probably the best collection there is anywhere) have now been brought back from the outlying villas where they were hidden during the war, and very few are missing. The two big Botticellis, *Venus* and *Spring*, get practically an entire room to themselves in the new arrangement of the gallery.

As for the villas themselves they have been more unlucky. Some of them have been destroyed, nearly all have been looted. One of the most famous of them, the Gamberaia at Settignano, was once lost at the gaming tables at Monte Carlo. It was in American hands before the war, but it was used as a storehouse for military maps and when the Germans came to leave they poured benzine over it. The place burned for several days and that, for the time being, was the end of one of the loveliest houses in Europe.

An incalculable wealth was poured into these places, especially in the early years of this century when Florence was probably the largest Anglo-American city in Europe. But now the British owners have no money, the Americans want to sell, and very few Italians have either the desire or the wealth to keep them up. Usually you will find one aged and dispirited gardener in the grounds where there were a dozen before.

A thin little colony of Anglo-American émigrés and Italian aristocrats hangs on in the shadow of these huge houses, like the last bees in a deserted hive; and the older ones at least try to keep the trappings of tradition against increasing odds: breakfast in bed at eleven, luncheon off the family plate at half-past one or two; then the siesta, tea in the garden and perhaps a drive or a little chamber music before it is time to dress for dinner. The younger ones tend to drift down to small apartments along the Arno and kill time somehow with endless bridge and little cocktail parties. Time, as Machiavelli wrote, no longer drives everything before it as in the days of Lorenzo the Magnificent. It hangs heavily over the rich in Florence, an inexhaustible fund of minutes, difficult to spend.

Yet still, for anyone who has a taste for domestic architecture in the grand manner, there is a marvellous appeal in these vast colonnaded entrance halls, the painted ceilings, the water gardens and the lines of classic statues shrinking away into groves of cypresses. It is not difficult to recall the great days when carriages came bowling up the gravel drives for balls that began at midnight and ended among a flurry of footmen and horses and dogs, and the scent of faded camellias in the morning.

And its not a little pathetic sometimes to go to one of these historic villas through unclipped hedges and dry fountains and find all the windows shuttered. For a long time after you have pulled the bellrope and heard the echoes of the bell inside no one answers. Then at last one is conducted across icy marble floors and through halls that have something more than just this winter's gloom, to a tiny suite of rooms on the second floor, the only heated part of the building. Nearly always it is the women who have outlived the men; and so one usually finds the *padrona* the Contessa this or that, an old lady of great but very fragile charm, encompassed by gilt chairs, an escritoire with a jade handled letter-opener on it, a cabinet full of Dresden ware, a basket for her dog, a row of books and, hanging about in the background somewhere, an ancient waiter wearing white muttoncloth gloves on his hands.

She peeps, as it were, over the edge of the last century, and not very willingly. Those terrible communists down in Florence...

Chapter Two

Lire, Soldi and Dinari

Portofino – the Port of the Dolphins – lies just south of Genoa, and it is notable for the fact that St George of the Dragon (or at least a generous portion of him) happens to be buried there; the place has a Lucullan kind of beauty of its own, something along the lines of Capri, or possibly Carmel, California. But for the first few years after the war the seasons were poor. The American tourists did not arrive. The British were allowed to bring only £35 out of England; (barely enough for a ten-day trip unless they happened to have a lucky break in the French casinos); and the Italians and the French themselves seemed to have baulked at the high prices and the ominous news about Russia.

Even the weather went on behaving in a way which the Italians describe as *squilibrata*, which means haywire or crazy,

Portofino

with perhaps a touch of malice in it. Along the Ligurian coast where normally one expects an idyllic atmosphere of fireflies in the warm night and casual luncheons in the sunshine, there were hardly two fine days together in May and June; and later on a series of operatic thunderstorms rushed down from the Apennines, smashing the young olives and the grapes on the vine. The local farmers tended to ascribe these upheavals to the atomic bomb. It was still an unusual and uneasy time, a sort of geo-physical depression between the Russian crisis and the arrival of Marshall Aid, with atmospheric accompaniments.

Many of the sailing boats were drawn up on the cobblestones of the piazza and had not touched the water for months. Some of the villagers were out of work. But it was possible once more to buy fish (the big hotels had cornered the whole catch the previous year), and the price of oil and pasta and one or two other things had come down. Domestic servants earned about four dollars a week, which is about the same as now. The half dozen shops in the village were full of unsold souvenirs and tourist gadgets and many a rich businessman's holiday villa remained with its blinds drawn and the shutters firmly closed. Up in Milan the bourse kept fluttering like a humming-bird because of the Russian crisis, and the businessmen did not care to stay away from it for more than a day or so.

Possibly the Portofino lace-makers and the boatmen were the most baulked of all. They were accustomed to sit under the arches in the piazza crying *'Comprare! Comprare!'*

and '*Barca! Barca!*' like a chorus in the opening number of a musical comedy; but this year they cast a wintry eye over the harassed English thirty-five-pounders and simply got on with what they are doing, which was usually discussing the local politics and the high cost of living. Politics, like the weather, had long since been treated by the villagers as an act of God, wholly unpredictable, and usually changing for the worse.

And yet despite all this Portofino remained on the surface incredibly and incurably gay, and the people were delightful to live with. Perhaps it was their superb talent for anarchy in local government, the gift of living from hand to mouth and from day to day. Perhaps it was their unconscious art of making themselves part of the landscape and simply accepting things as they were without feeling the slightest moral urge to improve them. Perhaps it was because they worked extremely hard. Perhaps, too, they were the only people in Europe, with the possible exception of the Greeks, who really knew how to play the role of poor relations, the worst role in the world, without any false pride or falling off of the national gusto. However, whatever it was, there existed a fine earthy squalor in Portofino and tourists or no tourists the villagers just let fly with a natural passion for vendettas, arguments, fiestas, ceremonies, weddings and funerals, most of which were conducted with the absolute maximum of violent colour and violent noise. The tragedy of life lay hidden quietly underneath.

The season got off to an excellent start with the celebration of St George's Day. Some three hundredweight of dynamite was exploded in the adjacent hills. There was nothing much to show for this – just a shattering and terrifying noise – but the entire village was delighted because it eclipsed any noise they had heard in recent years, and as such was regarded as a special mark of distinction for the saint.

One really has to know about St George before one gets a firm grip on affairs in Portofino. The local story of how he came to be buried here seems to square very fairly with the account set down by Gibbon in the *Decline and Fall of the Roman Empire*. According to this, St George was a Cappodochian meat contractor at the time of the Crusades in the Holy Land, and he may or may not have set upon the dragon in the ordinary way of business. At all events he rescued the maiden and was duly sanctified for the exploit. It was one of the later waves of crusaders who collected the remains of the saint and set sail from the Middle East on the return journey to England. Somewhere in the Mediterranean they ran into a storm which threatened to engulf the fleet, and they swore a vow that if ever they should make a landfall safely, there the bones of the saint should be deposited. The landfall was made in the tiny harbour of Portofino and they built a church in the village.

This is the point where the story takes an unexpected commercial twist, involving the Bank of England, the

Germans and eventually the RAF. It appears that the fame of St George soon spread some thirty kilometres up the coast to the City of Genoa, where a group of businessmen were engaged in starting a bank, actually the first bank in Europe. They needed some reassuring symbol to bring in the depositors. What could be better than the cross of St George and a picture of a horseman riding valiantly upon a dragon?

About this time the city merchants of London decided that they would like a bank too. They went down to Genoa and bought up the Italian Bank of St George, its banner and its symbol. They even took back to England the Italian practice of referring to lire, soldi and dinari as £ s. d. So English pounds, shillings and pence are known as £ s. d.; St George's Cross floats over the Bank of England; the figures of a horseman and a dragon are engraved on the Bank's golden sovereigns, and St George is now the patron saint of England as well as of Portofino.

The Portofino villagers were delighted to share the saint with England until an unhappy day towards the end of the war. An RAF bomber homeward bound after a raid on Italy picked off the village church with a single bomb and demolished it completely. It was not really a wilful act or even a bad shot; the Germans had ringed the place with anti-aircraft guns and the nearest lay only fifty yards away. But to the villagers it seemed that now, at last, the cataclysm had come. They ran in dismay through the smoke and rubble and when eventually the debris was cleared away it was found that a miracle had occurred; the tomb of St George in the crypt was intact.

Last year the rebuilding of the church began. And so the firing of three hundredweight of dynamite had a special significance for the village: St George was to be enshrined again to the noise of high explosive. And this would mean more fish, more tourists, more babies and less cause for alarm over Russia.

St George, then, is something super-added to the ordinary business of life in Portofino, and he is present on every possible occasion from a vendetta to a christening. When a youth skids on his motor-cycle and narrowly averts death at a railroad crossing he will, as like as not, have a lurid painting made of the incident and this he will hang up in the church as a tribute of thankfulness to St George. When a housewife descends into the piazza to do her shopping she will quite often pause at one of the little wooden shrines on the hillside and murmur a prayer that the price of olive oil may have come down. Even the communist is quite capable of invoking St George in his campaign against the capitalists. Whoever you are, St George is always on your side.

Because Portofino is a relatively prosperous village living off wealthy tourists for a great part of the year it did not follow by any means that all the villagers voted Right in the last elections. One would guess, at a venture, that about two-thirds supported de Gasperi and the Christian democrats. The rest were and still are communists. Communism does not necessarily represent for them atheism or Russian domination, but Portofino communism; a general share-out of things here in the village. They look at the millionaires' yachts and motor-boats in the harbour, they peep over the walls of the lavish tourist villas, they see a month's wage being spent on a dinner in a restaurant; and not unnaturally they compare all this with their own dark homes in the piazza and their jobs – if they are lucky enough to have jobs – which start at dawn and go on until after dusk. A workman's wage is about ten dollars a week. It is not much good warning him about the terrors of Soviet rule or asking him to observe the glories of free enterprise in a free society. Life for him is here and now in Portofino and it is still not good enough. St George himself must see that.

Seen from this angle Marshall Aid for Italy does not appear as a sufficient American gift to save the freedom of Europe, but rather as a lifebuoy which happens to be passing by in a stormy sea. One grabs it and starts looking round for something even more secure to get hold of. It will not be until later on when de Gasperi has really done something about unemployment, rising costs and low wages that the Italian worker in this or any other village will be able to draw breath and see where all the help is coming from.

Meanwhile the outward life of the village goes by pretty much as it has done since the Roman times. It is bound to the absolute routine of the grape crop in September and the olive crop in November. The fire-flies come in June and the crickets in July. The eight winds of Portofino blow as they blew on the crusaders, and they are called, as they have always been called, the Sirocco, Tramontana, Il Grigale, Il Ponente, Mezzo-giorno, Il Mare, Borrasca and Maestrale. The fishermen work according to the wind and usually at night. When the Tramontana comes down they set out, two men to a boat, each boat with a brilliant acetylene lamp on the bow. One man stands at the prow, and as the fish (who have been hunted for twenty centuries and have never learned wisdom) come swimming furiously towards the light, they are netted or speared with a sort of iron trident. On a good night you will see the fishermen's light dancing about for twenty miles along the coast and they evoke a curiously vivid impression of the traffic headlights passing up and down Fifth Avenue or the Champs Elysées on a winter's evening. In the morning the women dry the nets along the Roman flagstones of the mole.

Close by the postman stands as he has always stood in the centre of the piazza with his letters in his hand; he does not fatigue himself by climbing the rocky paths to the houses on the hills above. If the ratepayers happen to come down to the piazza they get their letters: if not, no. The children still go to bed at midnight well filled with spaghetti and wine. There is still the traditional adoration of babies and the ancient cruelty to animals. No cow ever gets out of its dark stall, from birth to death. There was a sensation when one escaped last year and, seeing the sunlight for the first time, frisked about so madly that it broke its leg.

It is still not safe to travel at night on the southward road to Spezia they say, because of the bandits lurking there. (Mild bandits, however. Once they grabbed a priest who was collecting funds for a foundling home. They took 10,000 lire from his purse but restored the money and added 10,000 of their own when the priest explained his mission.) And the old charm and courtesies persist. If a tourist remarks to a waiter that it is a fine day he is apt to get some such reply as: 'Ah signor it is always sunshine when you are here.' An English visitor who lives in a particularly lofty and beautiful villa was a good deal startled the other day by a piano tuner who had climbed the mountain to put the piano in order. When the Englishman came to ask for the bill the musician removed his hat and remarked with relish: 'But signor, how can I give you a bill when you are already living in heaven?' These pleasantries arrive with the regularity of the morning sunshine, and come, if not from the heart, at least from somewhere near it.

Given a routine like this the people have taken the various foreign invasions in their stride. The first wave of the English milords and eccentrics was a fairly easy thing to handle. It began somewhere about the middle of the last century when the fourth Earl of Carnarvon arrived on a mule and decided to create a summer pleasaunce beside the sea. He bought up the side of a mountain and the services of most of the eager peasantry round about. Being an aristocrat of independent spirit he chose to ignore the fact that the Carrara quarries lay only a few miles down the coast and were selling some of the most lovely marble in the world dirt cheap. Instead he sent off to England for a boatload of his native Portland cement and presently a large and monumental mansion rose on the cliffs, pale ginger in colour, and strictly Victorian in style, which was (and still is) something of a wonder in these parts. Nobody was restricting a British aristocrat to £35 in those days.

There followed other Britons and Americans of the same tradition, and tourists who noted in their Baedekers that Shelley had been drowned a little further down the coast, and Byron had passed by here on his last journey to Greece, and Dickens had described the neighbouring village of Camoglie as 'a most piratical sort of place'. The 1908 guide-books also warn the visitor that the local inn is 'unpretending', and that the nearby beaches are apt to be unpleasantly crowded on days of fiesta 'with the poorer sort'.

And then, still early in this century, there arrived the wave of painters, writers and musicians. Major Yeats Brown, who had a success with his book *Bengal Lancer*, established himself in an ancient castle on the headland, and soon the Castello Brown became a centre of mild inspiration for the arts. A perpetual house-party seems to have raged there in the lusher years before and after World War One. Emil Ludwig is said to have written some of his best works sitting upon the castle terrace. Elizabeth (of *Elizabeth and her German Garden*) achieved a volume about Portofino entitled *The Enchanted April*. Max Beerbohm set up house across the way at Rapallo; and there were many others, including American and British painters of the Sargent school.

But for some reason the artists have always been baffled at Portofino, and though at times a painter seems to be lurking under every bush around the village, no really worth while canvas has ever been produced. Possibly the scene is too crowded and the light too hopelessly fickle.

Most of Portofino is made up of a complicated mixture of vines and olives, of domestic pines, cypresses and stark brown rocks all tumbling down together over the terraced cliffs into the violent blue of the Mediterranean. It is fantastically picturesque but damned hard to get the thing down on canvas.

A Japanese artist arrived when we were there and used an approach which is certainly new and possibly requires some obscure form of Oriental thought transference. He seated himself with his easel and was observed to be concentrating upon one of the really tricky bits of the scenery, all flowers and vineyards and brightly coloured fishermen's boats along the mole. When some of the villagers went up to report progress on the work they saw with a good deal of expressed astonishment that the artist had painted an interior of a bedroom, something which might have served as an advertisement in a furniture manufacturer's catalogue. No such bedroom existed at any point of the landscape so far as the normal eye could see. Nevertheless the artist kept his eye implacably upon the nearest grove of cypresses while he filled in the colours of the bedroom carpet and the wash-basin. Then, with no more explanation than a pleasant smile, he folded his easel and went away.

After the artists and writers came World War Two and the Germans. They took Major Yeats Brown's collection of Tuscan pottery and flung it down into the harbour. They built an anti-invasion wall across the sea front and forbade all fishing. They moved into the English villas and constructed gun emplacements in the vineyards. It was an unusually large garrison for so tiny a place, but the German commander was apparently convinced that the Allied armies were about to follow up their Salerno and Anzio landings with a third and final swoop on Portofino, and thus complete the conquest of Northern Italy.

In actual fact the front line never reached the village; the Wehrmacht collapsed some distance to the south. But Portofino by then had endured two years of exceptionally repressive occupation. Some of the villagers whom the Nazis judged politically unreliable had been tortured and killed. Once a score of local boys who had joined the partisans in the hills were taken and shot in a bunch, and their bodies cast into the silent sea. By the time the first British and American troops drove into the piazza the flowers were heaped high about the monumental plaque which implores the passer-by to 'spare a flower, a thought for those who died.'

The final invasion of Portofino set in immediately after the liberation and this was the invasion of the Italian millionaires. They descended in shining motor cars from Genoa and Milan and immediately set about converting the old fishermen's homes into modern duplex apartments. Last year some of the English came back as well and the prices in the village shot up to the point where they became about the highest in Italy, barring perhaps Capri and Venice in the season.

One man drove an electric lift shaft down through the living rock so that he should not be fatigued by the five minutes' walk from his villa to the beach. It was the first wild spree of spending after six years of wartime dread and uncertainty, after twenty years of Fascist controls. If you had money (and many of the Milan businessmen had a lot of it, recently acquired) you spent it quickly; great broad vistas of peace, security and good business lay ahead. Nobody yet was thinking about a Russian crisis; nobody paused to reflect that political anarchy is not really the antidote to Fascist controls. This was the bright free time of the black market and government by laissez faire. It was each man for himself.

Some few controls did curiously survive this hectic moment, notably the power of the Department of Fine Arts. It may be true, as Stephen Spender said, that the Italians live like tourists in their own country, but they have made a special effort since the war to preserve its beauty and its irreplaceable art. The Department of Fine Arts tends to crack down fiercely when an exuberant merchant tries to run up a nice new gas-station in a fifteenth century piazza or starts advertising in neon lights on a Roman forum. The promontory of Portofino has long since been declared a national monument, and before you can build a new house there or even so much as add a spare room for the guests you must first get the approval of the Department. In fact they don't like new houses at all.

One of the Milan tycoons, apparently animated by the same spirit as the Fourth Earl of Carnarvon, decided to ignore all this. Fine Arts or no Fine Arts, he wanted a villa, so he had one built without permission on a nice terrace above the piazza. The roof was on and the furniture was about to go in when the officials of the Belle Arte arrived. They were not much pleased at having been defied in the first place and they were still less pleased when they saw the completed villa. They ordered the owner to take the thing away.

Normally in Italy there are ways of adjusting such little differences as this, especially if you are a big enough tycoon. This time there was no adjustment. The mayor and the villagers sided in a body with the officials. Indeed, it was a situation which made a strong appeal to the Portofino people in several ways; the demolishing of the villa would create more work for the local masons, and at the same time the village could congratulate itself on preserving the native beauties of the countryside. There may also have been a certain amount of pleasure in the thought that this was one occasion when the rich weren't going to get away with it, especially a rich foreigner from Milan. Then, too, the Italian has as much childish delight in smashing things up as any man in Europe. The dismantling of the villa was carried out with great gusto.

But it was the Americans whom the villagers were really waiting for. 'In the summer', they kept promising themselves, 'the Americans will arrive. Then we will have real prosperity.' A good deal of preparation was made during the winter. The leading hotel sprouted a new wing, a new motoring road was driven across the promontory (the Department of Fine Arts approving). The village bookshop laid in a stock of such representative American fiction as *Vita Con Papa* by Clarence Day, and *Il Postino Suona Siempre Due Volta* by James M. Cain. By early June many a new waiter in a starched white jacket flicked his napkin at the flies around the restaurant tables under the ilex trees, and the black market price of gasoline went up to four dollars a gallon, preferably payable in dollars. This was just three times the price of the local wine. At the end of June the hotels were still waiting for the American bookings. By July the village had given up hope. Instead of Americans they got the general strike.

One of the features of life in Italy these days is that nothing ever seems to happen quite rationally. There is a quality of fatalism and inevitability about the more serious events, a feeling that they have got beyond the reach of human control; they happen simply because they have to happen. And, quite often, before a really disastrous event, the villagers will discover portents and supernatural signs in the sky as though they had communicated to it some of their own restlessness and misgiving.

Directly they heard that Togliatti, the Communist leader, had been shot in Rome, they assumed that their lives would be thrown out of joint once more. There was no rational reason why there should be a general strike, but it was accepted at once as the most logical thing in the world. Political murder is the one sure sign in Italy that the country is coming to the boil, and it was almost as though everyone had been waiting for this special and inevitable incident. In Portofino the news was accompanied by a quite unprecedented summer storm. It came rushing out of the Ligurian sea and covered the whole coast with trailing wisps of fog and mist.

Nothing much happened on the first night except that the lights went out. The lights always go out in Italy at the slightest sign of trouble. Standing on the heights of Portofino one could watch the electric current fail for twenty miles along the coast. First the lights of Chiavari flickered and went black. Then Rapallo and Santa Margherita and so on through all the fishing hamlets up to Genoa until there was nothing left but the car headlights: and these soon vanished as well, leaving the whole coast in blackness and pouring rain.

At ten o'clock the following morning a dozen communists cycled into Portofino from Santa Margherita and peremptorily ordered all restaurants, hotels and shops to close, all work to cease. Only the food stores were permitted to remain open until midday. The communists had no authority to give these orders any more than the communists in Prague had any authority to take over the Czechoslovakian government. Nevertheless they were obeyed in just the same way. They were obeyed because the single policeman in the village had no power to prevent them and because Portofino itself contained a little cell of communists and the rest of the people were apathetic.

The communists were very thorough. They went to each shop and café in turn and ordered the shutters to be put up and the tables and chairs to be taken off the piazza. They did not bother to make the ten minutes steep walk up the hillside to the Restaurant Aurora but simply telephoned their instructions to the proprietor.

Only one villager resisted, an old lady of 82 who ran the Restaurant Delfino. 'Who are you to give me orders?' she cried. 'I'll open and close my restaurant whenever I like. Get out of the village. You don't belong here.' She made a great scene in the piazza, standing on the cobblestones in front of her house and shrilling at the communists at the top of her voice. The rest of the village looked on passively while the argument raged until at last the old lady was overborne. Her staff refused to work and so there was no point in opening her restaurant anyway.

The communists were ordinary young Italian workers from Santa Margherita and Rapallo, but they gave their orders with great seriousness and determination as though they had a religious purpose in what they were doing. Certainly there was no sense of humour in them.

'May I swim while the strike is on?' one of the English tourists asked mildly.

'You may,' one of the young men said, 'provided you do not have the appearance of enjoying yourself.' He said this quite seriously, and it was evident that he regarded this as a day of national crisis, when no decent man or woman would want to indulge in pleasure of any kind.

Having thus secured the village, and having made sure that the post office and the town hall were closed, the communists got on their bicycles and rode away. The whole operation had taken only an hour.

In the hotels the waiters held a hasty meeting and agreed to serve the resident guests provided they came early to their meals. The normal Italian sense of the comic and the ridiculous seemed to have died out in them as well; they resolutely took off their white jackets and their little numbered metal buttons, and as they served the guests they affected not to be waiters at all, but simply men who happened to be about the house and who were willing to lend a friendly hand in a crisis. This was a very strange performance.

Through the day no buses arrived in the village. We had no letters, no telegrams, no light, no electric heating, no newspapers and no news. An eerie quietness settled over the piazza and while the storm bashed itself against the

Piazza D'Esedra, Rome

cliffs the foreign tourists wandered disconsolately over the hills with little picnic baskets in their hands. It was evident that the village was quite powerless to conduct its own affairs. Ever since the arrival of the communists in the morning it had become numbed and atrophied; and any decision which was imposed upon it from outside would be accepted, any order from the communists would be obeyed. Possibly, the villagers might have taken a stronger line if they had had any news from the outside world, but there was no reliable news, only rumours of fighting in the streets in Genoa and Livorno.

It is this absence of news, this sense of isolation, which is the most corrupting thing about a political crisis. It creates a vacuum which splits the community into individuals, and the individual is left with no clear idea of how he should act for the best. He feels himself deserted and rudderless, not knowing whom to trust; and it is so hard to act alone. Rather he chooses the unheroic course of simply waiting to see what will happen. This is an atmosphere in which any strong political machine develops the strength of a giant and the communist boy suddenly finds himself a dictator because he is the only one in the community who has a plan, and a party behind him. The communist does not go on strike; it is when all the rest are idle that he becomes really active. He expands in a time of abnormality and achieves power and decision at the same rate as the community loses its normal will.

This, at any rate, was how things looked at the time. There was one interesting facet: the extraordinary outburst of affection among the workers for Togliatti, the Communist leader who had just been wounded. It was something akin to the feelings of the automobile workers in America when Reuther was assaulted in Detroit, but far wider and deeper than that. One wonders whether there would have been such a spontaneous outburst if it had been a leader on the Right Wing who was attacked, say de Gasperi, or some dignitary of the church. In other words the Left is producing its own martyrs in Italy and Europe these days. They have the authentic mystical glow for their followers. But where someone like Gandhi at his death creates peace, they create a riot.

So then Portofino, along with a thousand other villages in Italy, got through this strike without much distress and no bloodshed, and after a while resumed its normal habits again. The return of the hot sunshine coincided with the ending of the strike.

Yet quite clearly some damage is done to the collective village mind by these constant upheavals and upsets, an invisible damage like the decay or atrophy of certain cells in the human brain. The Italian peasant is peculiarly exposed because he suffers as much as anyone in Europe from a lack of loyalties. Half-way through the late war he was suddenly obliged to go into reverse when his government left the Germans and joined the Allied side. After the war there was still nothing much to which he could attach his faith. The central government was hopelessly weak. Its ration tickets meant nothing. Its bank-notes were inflated. Half its laws became submerged and lost in the seething black market.

Not unnaturally the village of Portofino did what nearly every other village in Italy did: it turned its back on the central government in Rome and went its own way. It ignored the ration tickets and the laws and even to some extent the inflationary bank-notes. A private system of barter sprang up. The village grew and ate its own food and wine, made its own clothes, repaired its own damaged bridges and houses. Life coalesced around the piazza and the family and the local saint. The big cities and the tormented politics lay somewhere over the hills, apart.

All this might have been very fine indeed, but neither the cities nor the politicians are willing to leave the village alone. Little by little it has been sucked into the main stream of the country's life by the Communists, by the Christian Democrats and Marshall Aid, by the menace of the Russians who lie barely a day's car drive away to the east, and in the last resort by its own helplessness.

During the strike Portofino went back naturally to the ancient ways of life. Since no trains or buses ran the villagers walked. They had no gasoline for their motor boats so they rowed. In the absence of electricity they cooked on charcoal fires, and lit their homes with candles. When the radio and the Press and the Post Office ceased to operate they exchanged information by word of mouth. In brief, the twentieth century with all its mechanised gadgets let them down and they returned easily enough to the old slow and primitive life.

Even now when things seem more settled in Italy they feel tolerably certain that something else, equally disagreeable, will turn up presently and the lights will go out again. Apart from St George, the only possible philosophy to have in these circum-stances is that it is a good thing to be on the winning side. If the Americans manage to save Italy, well and good. If the Russians get there first, not so good – but still they will have to be accepted, just as the Germans were. Somehow de Gasperi will have to establish a little more faith in his government before the villagers will bestir themselves in their own interests.

Meanwhile the ordinary economics of life keep breaking down and the situation is very wobbly indeed. One has the curious sensation that this little community is travelling back towards the last century before Carnarvon arrived; and perhaps beyond that, even back to the days when the Crusaders first came ashore in the little harbour. Conceivably, then, the villagers might be left alone with St George at last. Some of them are beginning to think it would not be such a bad idea at that.

Chapter Three

Victory for Snail

Chiocciola the Snail won the Palio at Siena in the July meeting in 1949, with Tartuca, the Tortoise, and Bruce, the Caterpillar, placed second and third, though they lost their jockeys just before the finish. One horse was killed, another treated for concussion and minor street fighting broke out among the crowd both on the night before the race and on the day itself. Taken all round, in fact, it seems to have been fairly representative of the kind of thing that has been going on here each summer for the last four or five hundred years.

The Palio, which is a painted silk flag depicting the Madonna with allegorical flourishes, is raced for every year on 2 July and 15 August. It is probably the oldest race meeting in the world and certainly the most uninhibited. Cesare Borgia won it on 15 August 1492, though not surprisingly, in view of his public and private record, a protest was put in by the Marquis of Mantua whose horse ran second.

Originally the meeting appears to have begun as a bullfight somewhere in the Middle Ages. Later it developed into a race of mounted buffaloes, with a tournament on the side involving swordsmen, wild beasts and dancing girls. Eventually, in the fifteenth century, it degenerated into the normal horse-race which is run to-day – that is to say, it is normal by local standards.

There is a parade in mediaeval costume which is one of the most spectacular things of the kind in Europe, a series of preliminary trials, and finally the horses go tearing three times round the lovely Piazza del Campo in the centre of Siena. The course is ridden bareback and casualties come high. There are two very steep inclines to negotiate, and one of these, the San Martino corner, is a death trap. Sometimes a horse will fly clean out of the piazza down the Via San Martino, and this has given rise to the old Sienese saying that anyone who is late or lost has 'gone to San Martino'.

It is a little difficult for a foreigner to get a really firm grip on the rules at first. As in *Alice Through the Looking Glass* or Samuel Butler's *Erewhon*, everything here is turned inside out and done precisely the opposite way to everywhere else.

There is no money on the race. The prize is the silken Palio itself. Far from being a secular affair, the meeting is consecrated and blessed by the church and the horses run for the honour of the Virgin Mary. On the other hand bribery and corruption come right out into the open; it is not the horse that counts, but the skill with which his backers have been able to seduce and browbeat his rivals. If a champion appears, he is immediately excluded by the judges, on the grounds that a champion is unfair; all the horses should be as nearly equal as possible. There are no private owners: each horse is sponsored by a different district of the city. Finally, in the race itself, it is the practice of the jockeys not to whip the horses, but each other, and sometimes very cruelly indeed.

The enthusiasm bordering on delirium with which the whole city takes part in these proceedings, nuns, bishops, politicians and merchants, is something which ought to make an interesting field study for the students of Mediterranean culture one of these days – perhaps UNESCO or the Rockfeller Foundation.

By the time I got down here the day before the race the excitement was already running high. In the usual way each of the 17 districts of Siena had announced their intention of competing. But since there is only room for ten horses to race in the piazza, seven of them had to be excluded by lot. An innocent child was produced and drew the names of the districts, which are all known by their traditional symbols, out of a glass urn. This time the districts of Giraffe, Shewolf, Owl, Unicorn, Eagle, Wave and Panther were excluded. The starters were, Caterpillar,

Porcupine, Goose, Seashell, Valdimontone, Tower, Snail, Wood, Tortoise and Dragon. Among these the Goose's horse looked about the best thing going, a fine bay nag with a record of 54 victories behind his district. But in Siena they don't like anyone to win a race too often. Goose was brought down heavily to the ground in one of the preliminary trials. Everyone agreed there had been no accident about it. Two rival jockeys in settlement of some private vendetta had simply tripped him up and now he was with the horse doctor suffering from concussion. This left just nine horses in the race and the major trial still to come.

A Professor Nerbi, in the horse-medicine and penicillin business, offered to show me around. He seemed to think Nicchio the Seashell now had a reasonable chance – 'Depending, of course,' Professor Nerbi said, 'on what bribes are given and what arrangements are made between the captains of the districts this evening.' He went on to explain that it was quite possible for two districts to arrange for their jockeys to bump the favourite off the course. They might do this simply for the hell of it or because they knew they had no chance themselves, and they wanted someone else to win. Indeed it was quite possible that a jockey who found himself on a poor animal would start lashing out with his whip at the other horses and the other jockeys before even the barrier went up on the simple principle that this was the last opportunity he would get. 'There is always a certain amount of confusion,' Professor Nerbi said. All this was apparently quite fair and prescribed for in the rules.

I asked about betting, but Professor Nerbi was against this. There was no betting on the race he said. Betting was held to be unworthy of an event that involved only the honour of the district and the glory of the Madonna. And anyway, since neither form nor breeding nor the jockey's skill had much to do with the result of the race, it was a little difficult to know just how to place your bets.

Towards evening, when the long shadows of the palaces and a slight breeze made the heat more bearable, everyone poured down the streets into the piazza to see the last major trial of the horses before the actual race on the morrow. Seashell looked a fairly unpromising beast for my money, but I was assured that there was nothing remarkable about this; Palio horses are not bloodstock, but simply average hacks gathered from the surrounding countryside. Each district has to accept whatever horse falls to it by lot, and since the same horses turn up each year again and again, it is quite possible that you may be racing an animal in August which was your deadly rival in July.

What one looks for in a Palio horse is robustness, weight and a certain sangfroid in times of crisis – just the qualities one imagines which were required in the mediaeval war-horse. Experience, too, is a big factor. Just as good wine is said to stir in the bottle each time the Spring comes round, some of the older Palio horses grow restless as July approaches, and they show great skill in buffeting for position while the race is on. There was one veteran called Folco who won many times and finally finished up a victor at the age of 18, mounted by a jockey a few months younger.

This time after a bad start Seashell ran a very nice course until he was hurled on to the rails near the judge's box on the second time round. It was difficult to see exactly how it happened, especially as the crowd immediately rushed on to the course and began fighting round the horse. When the police had straightened things out it was found that the animal had broken his leg. He was shot the following morning. The incident was regarded as a particularly bad omen for this Palio, since, for the first time in history, Seashell's team was captained this year by a woman, the Princess Minne Carafa di Roccella. Professor Nerbi and I found her later that evening presiding at an inquest, a fashionable woman in Parisian clothes, and all that district of Siena which is known as Seashell was sullen and silent with the shops shut and people arguing bitterly in the streets. The traditional eve of the race banquet, which is held in every district, had been cancelled.

We proceeded instead to the banquet of the Tortoise at the other end of the town, for the Tortoise now looked to be a pretty good thing for the next day.

Tortoise, a chestnut of six years, was padlocked inside a dark cellar with a guard outside. Since he was unaccustomed to sleeping or eating alone, he had been fixed up with a small foal for a stable companion, and a shrine to the

Madonna, with an electric lamp, had been adjusted over his loose box.

Upstairs, much the same thing was happening to the jockey, where the banquet was taking place amid banners and songs and sacred emblems. He came in, a small, restless young man with black side-whiskers, and taking off his coat, he began to eat *maccaroni alla Bolognese* at great speed at the head table. Professor Nerbi explained that, with no offence whatever intended, neither this nor any other jockey would be left unaccompanied in Siena this night. Two men from the district would walk with him wherever he went, sleep in the same room with him, and, finally, conduct him to the race on the morrow. Jockeys for the Palio are usually professionals from other parts of Italy (though there was once a negro riding and once a local country girl named Virginia). They are paid a fixed sum (something between five hundred and a thousand dollars) and, Professor Nerbi said, it was felt unwise to let them get in the way of any further temptation – as they certainly would do if they roamed around Siena alone. Any friendly arrangements that had to be made with opponents would be undertaken by the captains of the teams, and instructions passed on to the jockeys afterwards.

It is this complete cynicism with which the race is run – this bland assumption that all men are inherently bad – which probably gives the Palio its special fascination. Things are done here in the narrow streets of Siena on the night before the race which would make the stewards of a more northerly race-course blench with horror. And yet if a team wins by the most dubious means, this in no way affects the honour or the sanctity of the victory. The Italian words *onore* and *virtù* are, in fact, taken in the Renaissance or Machiavellian sense; they mean a mixture of ability, pride, virility and cunning. The end justifies the means and honour is not a subjective thing that comes from a man's inner conviction; it is entirely objective, a kind of prize, which you must seize by any method you can. Then, too, as Machiavelli says, crime has a certain grandeur of its own. Once the bewildered stranger grips this point he has probably gone a long way towards understanding not only what goes on at Siena, but at quite a few other places round the Mediterranean as well – and in other matters, such as politics.

The setting of the race at least is lovely. Just at this season of the year Siena glows with a curious rosy light and the air is full of the scent of hay and gardenias. When, in the evening, the windows of the slender grey palaces are draped with their cinquecento banners and coats of arms, and droves of excited boys and girls come singing through the crooked streets, it does not matter much how hot the day has been or how angry are the fist-fights that are going to develop later over the local wine. All the squares are full of vendors selling flags, toys, straw hats, coloured models of the horses and the riders, whistles, lemons and oranges packed with ice-cream, fans, shawls and flowers. Music flows everywhere. In this atmosphere the deplorable ethics of the race itself achieve a certain logic, and there is a light-hearted suggestion in the air that human beings are, in fact, both fallible and childish – and so they might as well relax and enjoy themselves.

The Palio itself is lodged beside the high altar in the cathedral for the night, among the candles and the ancient flags of the competitors. It is impossible for late-comers to get a hotel room and many people sleep in their cars or in the fields. They kept pouring into Siena all through the night and again on the following morning; at first the villagers from the surrounding countryside riding on bicycles and bullock carts and wearing wide flapping hats, and later the rich tourists from Rome, Florence and Venice.

By mid-afternoon, when the sun was overpowering, it hardly seemed possible that so much as a stray dog could be added to this mass. Siena's streets are some of the narrowest in Europe, and three hours before the race they were choked from wall to wall with jostling streams of people. It is a remarkable sight looking down on this from one of the old mediaeval towers; the people in the crowd become identical ants, and the general picture is of a network of small dark streams all flowing in upon one another until they burst out eventually into the open lake of the piazza. When you get into the crowd yourself you discover that there are many cross currents from the smaller alleys, and here and there a counter-stream, which for no apparent reason, except that a large number of people have spontaneously willed it, flows upward and away from the centre of the city.

In these circumstances the individual will does not count for very much. Among so many faces all faces become one face, and it is impossible to know whether you are being shoved by a blacksmith or a bishop. Indeed, some of the heaviest blows are delivered by nuns and frightened women. The same sweat runs down everybody's cheeks, and the smell of garlic makes a blanket over all. Women and children on the point of going down to the cobblestones are suddenly snatched up into the air again, and the noise of screams, shouts, laughter and shuffling feet is so close at hand and so continuous that, after a time, it becomes as unidentifiable as silence.

Around four in the afternoon the parade began. Each district begins by taking its horse to the local church to be blessed. The horse goes right in and is led up to the altar with his jockey beside him. If, as the Italian guide-books delicately put it, 'he is lacking in respect for the sacred place', this is regarded as a sign of sure good luck and immense enthusiasm sweeps his followers. Meanwhile the priest is sprinkling holy water and intoning in Latin: 'Let this animal receive Thy blessing, O Lord, whereby it may be preserved in body and freed from every harm by the intercession of the Blessed Anthony through Jesus Christ Our Lord. Amen'.

Up at the Tortoise Church where Professor Nerbi and I found ourselves clinging to the altar rail in the late afternoon, this ceremony went through very poorly. Not only did the horse fail to make an act of disrespect, but he jibbed away madly from the priest and ducked his head aside from the holy water. However, he steadied down when we got outside and the procession began to form up. The procession from each district is pretty much the same – a drummer goes in front, beating so furiously that the echoes bounce back and forth between the buildings until there is no distinction between the original drum-tap and the echo. Then come the two flag-throwers, who go through an elaborate dance, which they have been learning since childhood. They weave their flags back and forth across their bodies and between their legs, pivoting like picadors in a bullfight, until at last both flags shoot up thirty feet in the air together and the crowd roars with delight. Next come assorted men-at-arms, standard-bearers and a caparisoned parade horse ridden by the jockey in a steel headpiece which he is going to need by and by when the race gets started. The Palio horse itself follows on behind with a dazed and frightened eye.

All these people are dressed in costumes that date from the Middle Ages, when taste in men's clothes was a good deal more adventurous than it is now; and since the costumes are constantly being renewed in the finest velvets and silks, and the colours run to scarlets, emerald-greens, golds and cerulean blue, the whole thing hits the eye with the effect of a Diaghilhev ballet. It's a very pretty thing to see, provided you can draw breath to look at it, for at this stage of the proceedings something like chaos breaks out in the streets. From all 17 districts these processions pour into the centre of the city. They march straight into the packed crowds, which part, miraculously, like the Red Sea rolling back before the Israelites, until at last they reach the cathedral. Here the Cardinal leans out of an upper window of his palace and bestows another blessing. The Palio is brought from the high altar, mounted on a bullock cart with trumpeters, and the whole combined parade with flags fluttering and drums beating, moves down to the piazza.

Pictorially this is the climax of the day. This year some forty thousand people had gathered in the centre of the piazza (which is free) or perched themselves on wooden stands around the outside (four dollars a seat on the shady side). Many more were clinging to the turrets and battlements of the surrounding palaces and leaning at vertiginous angles from the windows. There was a great show of banners and armorial bearings from the buildings, and two airplanes kept flying by trying to parachute little packets of chocolates on the crowd and mostly missing. From the top of the Mangia, which is possibly the most beautiful tower in Europe, the huge bell was tolling. Down below a layer of rich yellow Sienese earth had been spread over on the paving stones of the course to make things easier on the horses' hooves: and at the San Martino corner there was a line of mattresses trussed up against the balustrades with an ambulance standing nearby.

For an hour and a half, from six to seven thirty, the course was filled with the parade, and the spectators were given an opportunity of cheering their favourites and cursing their opponents. The Seashell team went very sadly by with black crepe hanging from their helmets and carrying in a conch shell a hoof of their horse, which had been shot in the morning. On the other hand, Oca the Goose, who was thought to be much too badly injured to compete, appeared unexpectedly in the parade with the obvious intention of running. It was widely said, probably the truth, that he had been heavily doped.

Perhaps the best thing about this procession is that it really does appear to be part of the natural life of Siena. Since the people taking part are the descendants of the men who actually designed and wore these costumes some centuries ago, and lived in these same buildings and streets, they manage to avoid that slightly embarrassed air that seems to overtake the usual country pageant. They look as though they wear these incredibly gay clothes and buskins every day. It really does seem to be the most natural thing in the world for Giuseppe, the baker's boy, or Beppo, the bank clerk, to be standing there in high-heeled shoes, long woollen hose, a doublet of claret-coloured velvet with slit sleeves of lemon-yellow, a hawk's feather stuck in his cap and in his hand a silver hunting horn.

Only occasionally, when one of the performers has caught sight of his mother or perhaps a cousin among the spectators, the illusion of continuous history suddenly collapses. A grin spreads over the boy's face: '*Ciao* Mama! Anna-Maria! Look at me.' With a self-conscious smirk he points to his surcoat of cloth of gold and the amorial bearings on his helmet. He waves his shield awkwardly; and then it is apparent at once that he is nothing more than Beppo, the junior clerk who will be sitting at his desk at the Banco di Roma in the morning, dreaming of motor-cycles and Betty Grable.

The race follows directly on the parade, and it is always a haphazard business. This time it was worse than usual. Twice the horses were lined up, and when at last they got away at least three of them were facing in the wrong direction. From the first Snail shot out in front and never lost his lead after that. He was only seriously challenged on the third time round when Tortoise broke free of the field and came up at a terrific pace. Snail's jockey took one quick look behind and got his whip ready for action. Simultaneously another horse, possibly Caterpillar or Dragon, got out in front and quite deliberately sandwiched Tortoise against Snail. Tortoise's jockey miraculously held his balance and pulled around the outside, but they got him on the San Martino corner. He shot out of the saddle clean over the heads of the crowd and landed beside a bench of nuns. By now the course was in a fearful shambles with horses toppling over and colliding against one another and the crowd already jumping over the balustrades to get at the jockeys. Snail swept past the judges in great style with Tortoise and Caterpillar, both riderless, a length or two behind. Of the nine jockeys who entered the race only three reached the winning post.

It was Snail's forty-sixth victory. His followers were still celebrating on Tuscan wine at dawn the next morning. A month later the official celebration took place, when a banquet was held in the streets with the horse in the place of honour. He got a special ration of oats.

Chapter Four

A Slow Sweet Poison

With the possible exception of Manhattan, another crowded island in the sea, Venice is the one place I know where, outwardly, everything looks and behaves more or less as you expect it to do. One glance at the skyline and you immediately have the feeling that you have been here before.

This is a garden where all the flowers grow to the specifications in the catalogue, and nearly all the things they tell you about Venice in the travel agencies turn out to be entirely true. The sunsets this summer were still breaking over the lagoon, just as they have always been described and despite the American, British and Italian warships lying there. The pigeons still rise and wheel in panic as the mid-day sun goes off, and one still feeds them by hand with a photographer standing by and St Marks in the background. (Unless you happen to be Mr Robert Sherwood, who was having a terrible time this August. The Venice pigeons tend to fly at six foot one or two inches, just over the crowd's heads, and Mr Sherwood is six foot six inches. Unless he edged his way round the sides he spent most of his time in the piazza fending off the onrush of wings about his head.)

But the place does need peace and prosperity. Like any other city, built and displayed for pleasure, it seems to fold up when the tourists don't come, for it has had no real business life of its own since Napoleon ejected the last Doge, 142 years ago; it grows nothing, and, apart from a few minor crafts like lace-making and glass-blowing produces nothing. In winter, which is simply a killing of time, until the sunshine and the tourists come back again, the people prowl about the streets with long sad faces.

That was what it was like in 1939 the year when nearly all the rest of Europe was at war, but Italy not quite. The uncertainty had a deadly effect, almost as bad as war itself. One after another the last tourists crept away and the hotels began to close – and for how long nobody knew. Italian soldiers, with black cockerel feathers in their hats, appeared in the streets, and there were belligerent Fascist posters pasted up along the canals leading off the piazza. Everywhere Mussolini's dark jowl jutted out of pictures in the restaurants and the shop windows, reminding the people to fight, believe and obey.

Things were scarcely much better in the first few years directly after the war. Miraculously no bomb fell here, but most of the hotels were still closed or requisitioned by the Allied Armies. There was not much lighting in the streets or heat in the houses, and many of the palaces along the Grand Canal had that defeated look of buildings which have been neglected and unlived in for far too long. There is always a certain dankness in Venice, and it seemed to be creeping up the old walls as though at last the sea was going to reclaim the islands for itself again. A searchlight played over the Army stores on the mud flats at Mestre to keep the thieves at bay, but beyond that, the place was as deserted as a cemetery by eleven o'clock at night. And the gondoliers were on strike.

I remember Field-Marshal Kesselring, the German commander, was being tried as a war criminal in the old Assize Court just beyond the Rialto about that time – I am writing now of the winter of 1946–1947 – but even that barely drew a crowd of a dozen or so. To many Venetians the trial seemed pointless; they wanted life and carnivals and tourists again, not revenge.

For me, the one bright spot in Venice then was a certain Doctor Ognibene, a noted professional guide, who came to my hotel on the Molo to show me round the churches and galleries. He was a tall, rather distinguished-looking man, aged about fifty, wearing a raincoat buttoned up to his chin and carrying an umbrella. Everything had gone to ruin in Italy, he remarked gloomily as we walked round to

Feast Day

the Doge's Palace in the rain, and Venice itself was dying a slow death of stagnation. His wife was ill, but it was almost impossible to get her proper food or medicine – the prices were prohibitive.

The Doctor, however, rallied considerably once we got to the Palace. His voice cleared, his arms rose in dramatic gestures and he discoursed on Titian and Tintoretto in the grand manner with which he used to hold a party of thirty or forty distinguished visitors in the old days. 'Look,' he cried, 'at *Bacchus and Ariadne*, the most beautiful and passionate painting in the world, the most complete expression of love. But who bothers to come and see it any more?'

We had a pleasant few days going round together, and I might have stayed longer, only I had my pocket picked and developed a mild attack of food poisoning. The Doctor was more depressed than ever when I left. His wife was worse. The lira had been devalued again and refugees were pouring into the town making it impossible for anyone to find work. Up in the Assize Court the judges had reached their verdict on Kesselring; the penalty was death (though it was commuted to life imprisonment later on).

All this makes it something of a pleasure to report that since then a great deal has changed. The long sabbatical years in Venice are over.

The first person I called on, arriving in August last year, was Doctor Ognibene, and we fixed a rendezvous at Florian's. I was waiting for him there when he came striding through the crowd under the gallery. He was dressed in a neat blue suit and he looked ten years younger. He glowed like this new Venice itself. In half a dozen crisp sentences he explained that his wife had recovered and he himself was so busy as a guide that he could only pause for a few minutes. He was taking round parties of 30 at a time, he said – English-speaking people on one day, Swiss, Belgians and French on another. At 400 lire a head, this was bringing him in the equivalent of $120 a week, as long as the season lasted. Venice, he agreed, had returned to her great days of ten years ago, and had even eclipsed them.

Indeed, this is a point which is fairly obvious, from the moment you arrive now at the Piazza di Roma from the mainland. The first thing you notice is that they have erected red, yellow and green traffic lights on the canals to control the mass of gondolas and motor-launches going by. Then, as you get down towards the lower end of the Grand Canal, you come on a string of rebuilt, re-modelled or re-conditioned hotels, and in August most of them hadn't a room to spare until the season was over. The newest of these hotels is said to have 700 rooms, each with a radio, an unheard of thing in Italy. Even in some of the back streets leading off the piazza – the *calli*, the *fondamente* and the *rughe* – a number of cheap boarding houses has sprouted up and every other doorway leads into a restaurant.

The explanation, of course, is the unprecedented rush of tourists. After ten years of war and rather dreary convalescence in Europe, there seems to be a kind of tourist-hunger for Venice now – for the simple pleasure of seeing a place that is not functional or enterprising, but merely beautiful. At all events 60,000 visitors came here in July, and from then on they arrived at the rate of 2,000 a day. By Feragosto, the big Italian holiday in mid-August, there was scarcely room to feed the pigeons in the piazza.

Every week there is another exhibition, a congress or a festival, and both the race-track and the airfield have started up again out at the Lido.

Last year the City Council's take from the Casino (they get 70 per cent) was $1.75 million, and this year it will probably be more. On one Sunday alone in August they got $35,000. Largely as a result of this the city's ordinary budget has long since been balanced, and even with an increase of nearly a hundred thousand in population since 1939 nearly everybody for the moment has got some sort of a job. Everywhere one goes, one notices the effect of these better conditions in the appearance of the people and the clothes they wear.

Since 1946 Venice has had an extreme Left Wing Council, headed by a Communist Mayor, who was born in Sicily, and the communists have shown that they are just as keen on getting their hands on the tourists' money as anybody else. They have turned Venice into the most expensive place in Italy and there has been no nonsense about austerity. If you can pay, you can get anything you want. However, most of the tourists who are arriving now are of the serious sight-seeing kind.

They come for just three or four days and they spend this time, guide-book in hand, plodding faithfully round the churches and the galleries. You find them exclaiming and marvelling at it all and they are obviously delighted. They are mostly young people, Italians and foreigners about equally divided. They have no money for gondolas (which start at the minimum rate of a dollar fifty), but walk or take the *vaporetto*, and many of them carry their luggage in rucksacks over their backs. They are the ones to whom all the worst things happen. They get their pockets picked, they wait endlessly in stifling crowds for the cheaper and slower boats, they get the worst rate of exchange on their money, they lose their passports and they seldom have a hotel room booked, but instead, they lug their luggage round until they find a boarding house that is cheap enough. They are the initiators of a curious new traffic in cameras and cigarette cases, for it seems that many of them begin their Italian tour at Rome and Florence, and by the time they arrive at Venice their money has run out. And so they sell their cameras and odd bits of jewellery here in order to get home again. By the end of the season there is quite a pile of these trinkets in Venice, and many of them find their way south again to Rome to be sold, no doubt, to the incoming wave of tourists next year.

The younger and poorer Americans are possibly getting the worst of this deal, for it is difficult to shake the fixed conviction of Europeans that all Americans are permanently rich and probably gullible. They are all finding Europe much more expensive than they expected. There is always a supplement for something or other, and after you have paid 10 per cent or 15 per cent service charges on your hotel bill the staff still expects to be tipped.

Yet despite all this, despite the waiting, the ennui and the scribbling of anxious little lists of expenses on the backs of envelopes, these earnest travellers probably enjoy themselves more than the others, and for them, perhaps, the thing is even better in retrospect.

But it is the rich and the half-rich, the people who are a straight recrudescence of the twenties, on whom Venice is really depending. They come here for fun with a little culture on the side – three hours on the beach and half an hour among the Tintorettos. They are the logical descendants of the cosmopolitan families who used to take a palazzo or a hotel suite for the season, together with a private gondola and a *cabina* on the Lido; and the Venetians love them dearly. They spend money with a rich and steady appetite. This summer when the International Film Festival was raging at the Lido, there were days when a kind of Eastern splendour reigned. Executives swept by in clouds of beautiful women to their couches on the beach. Behind each executive a sort of tented pavilion rose up on the sand, and the executive himself, as he lay basking, was girt with coloured cushions and screens to keep the sun and wind at bay. Here he was pursued by international telephone calls and aperitifs and men selling baskets of peaches and strawberries. Presently the secretaries, wives and daughters emerged from the pavilions wearing bathing suits of the least inhibited design; and a beach inspector, probably a communist, cast a moody eye over it all and did nothing. The effect was Augustan, Arabic and Californian all combined, and undeniably gay.

Towards half-past one or two the beach life streamed towards the cocktail bars among baroque columns (circa 1920) on the terraces above. And so to lunch at a quarter to three.

Film showings began at five and again at half-past nine or so, in a special festival theatre, bedecked not unlike a United Nations Conference Hall, with the flags of all nations this side of the Iron Curtain.

After that there were the night clubs and the casino, both prepared to carry on all night if necessary.

For a man not connected with the industry it was a little difficult to understand this festival. With the exception of *The Snake Pit*, a German production called *Berliner Ballade* and one or two others, most of the films were a commonplace lot. I asked a man in the publicity department if the competing nations did not seriously want to win. 'Why yes' he said, '*everyone* got a prize last year.'

'So there is no point in any nation showing its best films?'

'Well no,' he said. 'A good film gets publicity anyway. But if you show a poor film here, and it gets a prize, you get a nice lot of publicity you wouldn't get otherwise.'

Thinking this over uneasily for a bit he corrected himself. 'No, it isn't quite like that. There was a lot of lobbying went on last year, and this time it's all cleaned up. There are just going to be three main prizes: the first is a model of the winged lion of Venice, the second is a model of St George and the Dragon, and the third is a miniature of that big brass ball they've got stuck up at the end of the Grand Canal. And this year we have a jury of distinguished Italian critics and a priest. We found that an international jury wasn't much good, because its members tended to vote for their own country's films. Especially the Russian member.'

'I still don't understand,' I said, 'what everyone except the jury is doing here – the executives and the secretaries and so on.'

'Well,' he said, 'A lot of them are guests of the festival and they're staying here free.'

Apparently the Italian authorities find it good business to do this for the movie people attract large numbers of visitors. In a country so poor and disenchanted as Italy, the movie star has a double glamour – she is not only beautiful and famous, she is also inexpressibly rich. As she steps into her launch trailing flowers and attendants, the Venetians look down from the cinquecento bridge above without visible envy or resentment. They seem rather to be pleased that a human being can reach such heights of luxury and splendour.

There is another group of visitors here, the old habitués, and they avoid both the movie crowd and the tourists as much as they possibly can. These are the people who owned the palaces along the Grand Canal before the war and own them still. They are much diminished in numbers now, but a little coterie has hung on unmoved by dictators, wars, business recessions and the devaluation of the lira. They move in elaborate patterns from dinner party to dinner party exhaling a faint perfume of the Byronic days – the personal gondolier in his scarlet livery, the music in secluded gardens in the moonlight, a box at the opera, a champagne picnic at Torcello, and always, somewhere in the thick of it, the dominant young matron surrounded by her *cavalieri servanti*. The language is French and the wealth is boundless. 'My problem,' one of them remarked pleasantly one day, 'is not how to make money, but how to spend it.'

There is a certain fragile permanency about these families. Most people believed that the war and divided loyalties would ruin them. It was also a reasonable bet that their palaces would decay and become uninhabitable through disuse. Certainly some of the older buildings have developed a dangerous sagging and the city council is repairing them to serve as municipal buildings and museums. Others are being converted into hotels. But, in fact, the private palaces have not fallen down. They are said to be sinking at the rate of a yard every five hundred years, and at many of them you no longer step out on to a marble landing stage, but directly into the house. Most of Venice is built upon wooden piles driven into the mud, and these piles are slowly rotting, especially at the point where they are exposed to the air and the action of the waves set up by motor boats. But there is a method of filling the piles with concrete, and anyway the buildings seem to support themselves by leaning against one another, and the general facade along the Grand Canal is much as it was last century. The canals, too, are gradually silting up and there has been much dredging since the war. It is said to take ten years for the dredgers to go right round the city's one hundred and sixty waterways, and some of these are so shallow you can wade in them.

Probably it is the traffic that has altered more than the buildings. Although a gondola costs only $600 to buy, there are barely half a dozen privately owned ones left in use – chiefly because of the expense of the gondoliers who have a very tough union indeed. There remain the public gondolas, a sort of super-taxi service, the *traghetti*, which ferry you across the Grand Canal at ten lira a time, the tradesmen's gondolas, very squat and heavy, and even the hearse-gondolas in black and gold, which will carry you out to the island cemetery to be buried among flower gardens of multi-coloured glass. But nearly all the rest is motor-boats – the red ones of the fire brigade, with brass horses mounted in the prow, the small and noisy, and the large and silent, the *vaporetti* and the motorised canoes, and, latterly, a Coca-Cola motor launch with the crew dressed in the company's uniforms.

Naturally, there has been an outcry about this. There is a strong and fierce group of the old regime who deplore the Coca-Cola launch and the new advertisements on the bridges and the landing stages; and they are maddened by the new building which has been put up by the Daniele Hotel, alongside the Doge's Palace, on the most famous part of the waterfront. The Communist Council seems to be stepping cautiously through this controversy, with one eye on the cash and the other on the elections, which are coming up in the Spring. And, on the whole, even their enemies admit they have done pretty well in keeping the twentieth century at bay or at any rate under control. They are sponsoring a move to create a winter gambling season by moving the Casino, directly the fall is over, into the Vendramin Calergi Palace on the Grand Canal, where Wagner died. At the same time they have resisted an attempt to abolish the gondolas.

A good deal of this policy is the work of Professor Carlo Izzo, the *Assessore alle Belle Arte*, and the member for Tourism on the Council. The Professor is a deft and able little man, one of Italy's best scholars in English literature, a Neapolitan and a socialist of the Far Left.

When I mentioned the Daniele Hotel to him he exclaimed, 'How can you complain of a pimple on such a face?' – and went on more soberly to argue that at least the new building was something in its own right and not a cheap imitation of the lovely Gothic and Byzantine palaces higher up the Canal. 'Anyway,' he added, 'taste changes. There was a violent public protest against Longhena's Santa Maria della Salute, when it was erected in the seventeenth century, and

Outside the Quirinal

now we regard it as one of the most beautiful churches in Venice.'

About the future of communist Venice the Professor was not so sure. 'We were elected,' he said, 'in 1946 when everyone hated the Fascists and the Communists were their chief opponents. Now fascism doesn't seem to be hated nearly so much, and we may not get in again.'

Professor Izzo has just finished an Italian translation of contemporary American poets, and is about to embark on a British volume (putting Eliot among the Americans and Auden among the British, despite their change of nationalities). Meanwhile, he projects and presides over the twenty big exhibitions and festivals which Venice is holding this year. They have been nicely timed and arranged to rope in every class of tourist. During this summer if one was not moved by the Film Festival, nor ancient Sardinian bronzes, nor yet by the pigeon shooting competition or the regatta for young men in skiffs with one oar, there was always the Giovanni Bellini exhibition in the Doge's Palace.

This was something of a venture for the City Council. After many months of correspondence they got together some 140 of the master's works, many of them flown by air from America, England and France. What with the heavy insurance, the framing, and the fact that Bellini painted on wood (which greatly increased the cost of transport) the Council was about forty thousand dollars out of pocket by the time the exhibition was set up. And of this they cannot hope to get back more than thirty thousand, even by charging two dollars for a catalogue, which is much too much for most visitors. But it is an austere and lovely show. Many of the altar pieces which have been secluded in dark churches, lesser known works like the *Presentation at the Temple* from the Stampalia Foundation, and others from such private collections as Count Bonacossi's at Florence, have been cleaned and displayed together here for the first time in memory. The gentle and beautiful boy's head from the Birmingham gallery in England had not been seen on the Continent before this for many years. Both the *Sacra Conversazione* from the Uffizi and the *Transfiguration* from Naples are also shown.

This exhibition, the focus of the season, is being followed by such confusing items as opera in the open air, an aircraft race, a meeting of the Pen Club, a Toscanini concert, and an International Festival and Congress of the Dance, Popular Music and Song. For this last manifestation, 2,000 performers were invited from 40 different countries, on the understanding that they would wear national costumes in the streets and canals of Venice throughout their stay. At this writing, the phenomenon of parading say, a couple of hundred Highland pipers, Spanish bullfighters and perhaps American Red Indians in the Piazza San Marco has not yet taken place, but it seems hardly likely to fail.

But the real moments of Venice this year were undoubtedly the ancient festivals in the evening when the people poured out on to the Piazza San Marco and the canals to listen to their own music and singing. There was one night – 20

August – which is simply called 'A cool night on the Canal,' and has no other object but to allow people to be cool and enjoy themselves, when all the great palaces were floodlit and the bridges hung with lamps. Motor-boat traffic was stopped and the gondolas, each trimmed with coloured lights and bunting, came streaming into the Grand Canal in such numbers that they were locked together from bank to bank, making a bridge across which one might have walked. Towards midnight a large barge bearing a full concert orchestra, under a cupola of scarlet lights, came floating down from the Rialto. The gondolas clustered round the barge, and for the next few hours the crowds lay back in their boats watching the palaces glide by and listening to the music. There was a curious soft echo coming off the water in this narrow space until at last the whole mass of gondolas drifted out into the open lagoon in the early morning.

There is another time in Venice when the crowds come to listen to an open-air concert in the Piazza San Marco, and the people lean from the balconies or spread themselves among the café tables and the chairs. This is the moment, late on a mid-summer evening, when the moon is coming up behind St Mark's, making the gold turn green. All the surrounding buildings are linked by a chain of lights, and the piazza then takes on the appearance of a ballroom of fantastic size and beauty. This is the Venice of the romantic tradition; and it has a quite overwhelming charm.

One might have thought that something new would have been added by the war – that the visitors for example might have made some sort of morbid shrine of the villa where Mussolini and Hitler had their first meeting on the mainland just out of the town. But nothing like that has happened. Instead, one wanders about recognising the Rialto, the Campanile, the Bridge of Sighs, and all the other familiar things which are part of some forgotten fund of one's memory that probably started back in the schoolroom with Shakespeare's *Merchant of Venice*. It is all so untouched, so concentrated, so exactly what one would have wanted Venice to be.

And after three days of it, there are some people who just can't stand it any more. They become afflicted by a sharp attack of claustrophobia, the walls appear to be folding in and they have just one idea – to escape from all this beauty and get their feet back on the ugly solid mainland again.

This is an overpowering sensation, and it is not necessarily improved by a good night's sleep or a lucky break at the Casino. You wake one morning and Venice appears to have suddenly shrunken in the night so that it is not even an island but a ship – and a ship that is moored to the wharf at that.

For these people too (and there are a good number of them), Venice is just plain unlucky. Nothing very dramatic happens – just a series of little incidents; one misses one's train, one develops an irritating little illness, a suitcase disappears, a distressing letter arrives. One after another these misadventures occur with a quiet mysterious persistence. In the end the embattled traveller is left with an uneasy feeling that the city is bewitched and, like the demons in the trecento primitives, unseen things are striking at him from the darkness somewhere. It is all a little eerie, reminding one distinctly of Thomas Mann's short story *Death in Venice*. There is a cycle of love and death, so the superstition runs; those are the two things that are certain to happen in Venice if you stay long enough.

In pursuit of this mystery I took a gondola out to the island of San Michele and discovered that there is a sharp contrast with the rest of Italy in the way the Venetians bury their dead. No lavish mausoleums or marble sculptures rise up here as in most other Italian cemeteries. Instead, the dead lie in long neat rows, with little undemonstrative tombstones, standing barely a foot from the ground. Apart from the artificial flowers of coloured glass the whole island bears a resemblance to a military cemetery, as though the people wanted to make as little parade of death as possible. And, indeed, in one place you come on several rows of crosses which are even severer than the rest. This is where the German soldiers who died in Venice in the war are lying, mostly boys of 19 or even younger. They could hardly have been killed in action since there was no action to speak of in Venice. It seems instead that many of them died in accidents and through plague and in other ways that are not explained. And some who are buried without a name were simply found washed up on the edge of the lagoon.

Eventually I approached Professor Izzo on this matter of death in Venice and he nodded understandingly.

'Venice,' he began, and God knows he surely had nothing to gain in telling me the truth, 'is a slow sweet poison.'

There were many ways of trying to explain it he thought. On the whole Venice has a pretty beastly climate, full of rain and cold outside the tourist season; and this must have a lowering effect on certain natures. Then, too, there is a certain unreality about a place where the streets are filled with water, where there are so many strangers and so few trees and animals and children. (For some reason the tourists don't appear to bring their children. Off-hand I can hardly remember seeing a child in the piazza on the days I passed through, except for one reckless boy mounted on a bicycle, who was trying to mow down the pigeons beneath the Campanile. He was arrested.)

Everything is a persistent looking back to the architecture, the painting and the power of the Doges in the Renaissance, when Venice controlled an empire reaching to Turkey and commanded the largest fleet at sea. Over the last century or so nothing very much has happened here – nothing very great in the way of philosophy, music, painting, sculpture, poetry or writing, with the possible exception of the work of Goldoni, a minor Sheridan among the playwrights.

Even the Venetians themselves have the air of custodians of an institution rather than the residents of a city. They have only this one industry of the tourists, who come and go like the Adriatic tides. For the rest they say it is not the individual that counts, but the city itself, and the life that keeps turning over and over, year after year, in much the same way, creating one supposes, a slow fascination. One festival follows another and always on the precise date. Even the crime does not alter. Men still lurk in the crowded Merceria and the Largo Marzo playing the same old roll of cloth trick – upwards of a dozen people were caught by it in the last two weeks. Drunken men still fall into the canals at night and drown. The same kind of collisions occur – a Swiss family seated in a gondola was sliced in two by a passing motor launch the other day.

If, after being enticed on from one exquisite back street to another, the visitor is lost in Venice, there is one unfailing thing for him to do, the traditional thing – to get into the main current of the passers-by and inevitably it will carry him back to the Rialto again.

It all goes by on a fixed and definite rhythm. To some extent then, the people who are living here admit they often feel like caretakers in a vast, beautiful and decaying house. And most of them declare they love the place and will never leave it. Bewitched or not, they intend to stay here till they die.

Chapter Five

Bangs, Roars, Shrieks and Sighs

After you have been living in Italy for a while, you discover that life tends to go by on a certain fixed rhythm that is not at all like other places. January and February, for instance, are the months for political demonstrations and crises in the de Gasperi Cabinet. In March we usually get a breakdown in the electric current: and this is the month when a thousand little workshops start manufacturing religious souvenirs and alabaster models of the Leaning Tower of Pisa, which will be sold to the tourists by and by. April and May bring the music festivals, the nightingales and the fireflies; and round about June the hotels and the railways usually go on strike. For some reason this is also the season for bandits to start operating again in Calabria and Sicily.

July, August and September are the tourist months, when prices are increased by 50 per cent, and they keep moving steadily upward, until we arrive at October, when the grapes and the olives are ripening and Italy returns to herself again. During the grape festival the village fountains still sometimes run with wine, and ox-carts full of singing peasants come bumping down the valleys in much the same way as they did a couple of thousand years ago.

In Tuscany where I live, it is the custom for one man to begin a song by inventing a line ending in the name of a flower. He is answered from across the valley by a singer in another ox-cart, and traditionally this second line must end with an assonance. The third line is thought up by still another singer in another ox-cart and he has to produce a rhyme for the name of the flower. They do this, *allegro* and *fortissimo*, always singing impromptu three-line verses; and so it goes on to the accompaniment of harmonicas through the night. Altogether, autumn is one of the nicest times of the year in Italy, even when the Tramontana wind comes rushing down from the Appenines again. Then our winter starts in November, and it is often a good deal colder than England and even sometimes wetter.

But not last year. An almost unprecedented thing happened. For three solid months, early in 1949, scarcely a drop of rain fell from the sky. We got into difficulties at the Villa Diana almost at once, for we depend entirely upon wells which are filled by rainwater draining down through the subsoil from the top of Fiesole. Some of these wells are very old, and I have never yet discovered just how many there are – some are scattered through the farm and there are others in the cellars of the house itself, dark echoing holes that descend beyond the beam of an electric torch, and, sometimes, one hears noises down there, the dry scuttle of a lizard's feet, or a rat scampering, or perhaps, the whisper of a bat. One morning Anunzio suddenly announced that all these wells had dried up.

'I have been expecting it,' he said, 'for a fortnight.'

In Italy, after a little time, you no longer exclaim: 'But why didn't you warn us, so that we could do something about it?' In my part of the country few people will willingly volunteer bad news or tell you things that they think you do not want to hear. This is not weakness or irresponsibility: it is part of good manners. I phoned the engineer in the town hall at Fiesole, and he promised to lay on the municipal water supply at once. *Subito*, he said. Now in Tuscany everyone says *subito*, and no one ever comes at once. An elaborate game goes on and you have to know the rules if you are going to get anything done. In a country so poor as this everyone is constantly wanting something urgently and demanding it urgently. The man who makes a request in a calm dispassionate voice is simply a man who doesn't care. You must start on a really desperate note and work up from there; detached logic will get you nowhere and sarcasm is useless. The thing to do is to reach a certain flash point of agitation and then things go with a bound and a gallop.

The Road to Rome: Anno Santo 1950

It wasn't long before our drains became blocked. The earth under the olive trees cracked into flat dry slabs like huge biscuits just taken from the oven. Our tortoise, who would never normally think of appearing from his winter den until late July, was already pacing the terraces in April. The Contadino's Boy even reported that our larger tortoise, who is the size of a cushion, and who only appears, infinitely fatigued, every three years, had been sighted among the vineyards 12 months before his time. The box hedges, the sturdiest of all our plants, turned brown and died. One of the canaries had a heat-stroke. All this in the month of April, when the rain has been known to come down for 14 days on end; and for us it was doubly worse, because we had sickness in the house, and it's an exhausting business caring for a patient without running water.

I marched into the municipal engineer's office at Fiesole and rose to boiling point without an effort. It's that mortal cry of despair that always brings results in Italy. *E già fatto*, said the engineer, which means, euphemistically, it is already done, and when a man says that, you know you are getting somewhere. We had the water on within a week.

For us then, inside the house, the situation was saved, but for the farm and the surrounding countryside the situation was appalling. The wheat fields had crumbled into dust, and since most of the country's power is supplied hydraulically, the electricity was cut off, first one day a week, then two, then three; and at some places even more. Many thousands were thrown out of work because the factories ceased operating, and in Florence it was a familiar thing to see the clerks in the city offices crouching over their desks in candle light. A horrible kind of dankness – that combination of wetness and no light – crept into the buildings, and in the absence of lifts, people groped their way upstairs with lamps and torches like pilgrims on Athos. I was having some teeth stopped at that time and my dentist got out a hand-worked drill, a homely sort of device, looking like an early spinning wheel. He pumped away with his foot and the thing emitted a not unpleasant whirring noise, much less alarming than an electric drill; but it took an intolerable amount of time for him to make a hole.

In these trying conditions a good deal of attention was fixed on the Easter ceremony in the cathedral in Florence. This is one of the big occasions in Tuscany. Each year on Easter Saturday a wire is stretched from the high altar down the nave and out through the main door to a kind of wooden pagoda, which is erected on the piazza, outside just in front of the Baptistery. At the conclusion of High Mass, a projectile, which is supposed to be fashioned in the shape of a dove, comes whizzing out of the dark cathedral along this wire, rather like one of those gadgets they used to have in department stores years ago for getting change from the cash desk to the customer. This dove strikes the pagoda with a terrific bang, and if all goes well, it ignites a chain of fireworks there. Catherine wheels and rockets come spurting through the crowd, and the spectacle reaches its zenith with clouds of green, yellow and red smoke pouring out of the roof of the pagoda, to the heights of the Baptistery. The people pack the piazza in dense crowds to watch these proceedings, since, if the fireworks go off readily, then it's a sure sign there will be good crops and abundant rainfall for the remainder of the year.

This Easter it went through to perfection. The noise and the confusion were stupefying. Even the pagoda itself caught fire and a Florentine fireman, who was secreted inside, in case of accidents, was painfully burned. But not a thing happened to the weather.

Easter Sunday was hot and sunny, and so was the rest of all that week. The peasants looked up at the brassy sky muttering that it was now too late anyway, they were ruined.

But there is one more miracle in Florence; at the Church of Santissima Annunziata there is a Madonna, a painted fresco, which is unveiled only on rare occasions, and when it is, rain and good fortune follow. It was still a cloudless day when, about a week after Easter, the people went down on a pilgrimage to the Annunziata, and the ceremony was performed. I was not there, but I know for a fact that the clouds came up that night. They spread over the whole Arno valley with a dead heavy greyness, and then the rain came.

Since then – and I am writing about last Easter, not this one – we have had splendid rains in Tuscany. And the rest of the year's programme went through all right. We had the music festivals and the nightingales in May, and in June there was a little difficulty with the waiters in the big hotels in Rome. Down in Sicily the bandit Giuliano began murdering a few more *carabinieri*. By July the rentals of three-room apartments in the Via Veneto in Rome had gone up to $300 a month, and the tourists began to arrive.

Now Rome is already an overcrowded city. In these last few years it has altered from a leisurely Mediterranean place into a boom town, a sort of Coney Island of free enterprise. The official life of the city gathers round the government, and the double diplomatic corps (one part accredited to the Holy See and the other part to the Republic). But since the war there has been added an Anglo-American-Italian movie colony (it is cheaper to produce movies in Italy than almost anywhere else), and a group of international agencies like ERP, who maintain a surprising number of secretaries. On top of this there has been a wave of tourists and students which eclipses anything Italy has ever seen before and it goes on steadily increasing.

To cope with the rush, a building boom began, the biggest thing since Mussolini captured Ethiopia and won the Spanish war. Half a dozen new hotels sprang up and a hundred little *trattorie* sprouted out of the ancient walls, with bright new canvas blinds and privet hedges round the pavement tables. Among the lush plates of octopus and crayfish in the windows there is usually a card which announces: '*Ici on parle Français*' and '*English spoken*'. Select restaurants, like Alfredo's, where Alfredo himself used to prepare the *fettucine* and whirl his flaming *crêpes suzettes* round his head, have expanded into major feeding-houses with glossy panelling and hordes of waiters on the run. There are two English speaking movie theatres, an English language newspaper, and from the Piazza di Spagna to St Peter's, every bookstall sells every kind of American magazine.

In the Via Amendola which runs up from the Piazza Barberini to the Piazza San Bernardo there is a new chain of airline booking offices; and somehow, more than anything else, more even than the movie advertisements, they make you feel how much Rome has broken with the past. Airline booking office art is probably an international cult these days, and there is no getting away from it anywhere. But it looks strange here among the baroque Churches; those tubular steel chairs, the strip lighting in relentless shades of mauve and bluish-white, the glass placards suspended like bird-cages from the ceiling, and all those cute advertising signs, the streamlined sea-horses and sea-gulls, the flying pegasuses and the comic hotel porters with wings. Somehow that fearfully bright laboratory-like atmosphere, half functional and half fey, just does not go with Rome. But it is murals in the Via Amendola that really catch the eye. Strictly speaking, according to airline booking office standards, they ought to be allegorical with a touch of Picasso, but the Roman artists have struck out on a line of their own. They favour a superabundance of romantic nudes, or more simply Venus herself, rising from a Botticelli sea-shell and blown upon by four virile characters in billowing togas representing the four winds.

The other big change in the streets is the traffic. By last summer Rome must certainly have become the noisiest city in the world. Even before the tourists arrived, the Romans themselves produced a certain volume of bangs, roars, shrieks and street cries. But by September the traffic had increased 75 per cent. It was not so much the big American cars that got themselves stuck in the back alleys along the Tiber, nor yet the new half-size motor-cycles known as Wasps, nor even the terrified cries of the pedestrians; it was the ordinary push-bike to which was attached a tiny motor, just powerful enough to get the rider up the milder slopes of the city's seven hills. When one of these contraptions passes between the echoing travertine walls of the palaces, the noise achieves an annihilating quality that suspends all thought, like an electric shock, and seems to make life itself stand still. The manufacturers hoped to get many more of these bicycles on the road for the Holy Year.

Looking back, one sees it was the Americanisation of Rome and the big Italian cities which was the big achievement of last summer. To make and spend money fast, to work hard, to live on the moment, to put one's faith in the man rather than the tradition and skip the bureaucracy if you can – the city Italians were already eager for all this and the American executives flying over from New York by TWA showed them the way.

The de Gasperi reforms have, as yet, done nothing much to reduce the two million unemployed or bridge the gulf between the very rich and the very poor. It is still the accepted thing that the rich should evade their taxes and the poor are far too poor to be worth while taxing anyway. But you have got to admit that there is enthusiasm in the air. The small tradesman does feel that any day he may get his hands on some of those easy dollars flying around, and once on the ladder, it is only a short step towards an Alfa Romeo car and a villa at Capri. There were some wonderful parties in Rome and Milan last year. At one ball the guests arrived around midnight to find that all the reception rooms of the palace had been draped in tent-like hangings and lit by specially-constructed white chandeliers with scarlet candles. The champagne-whisky buffet (whisky at $16 a bottle) went on till morning, and there were 14 film stars and eight princesses among the guests, all in fabulous jewels and dresses. The communists might growl at the gaming houses where an industrial tycoon will lose five or six million lire in a night's play, but there is no real agitation about this. To live and live now – that is the big thing.

Co-incidentally with this, the movies, more particularly American movies, have gripped Rome with a passion that can hardly have been seen since the days of the chariot races and the circuses in the Coliseum. In the centre of the city every other street flames with advertisements. Visiting stars like Orson Welles and Tyrone Power, who have been around for the last year or two are referred

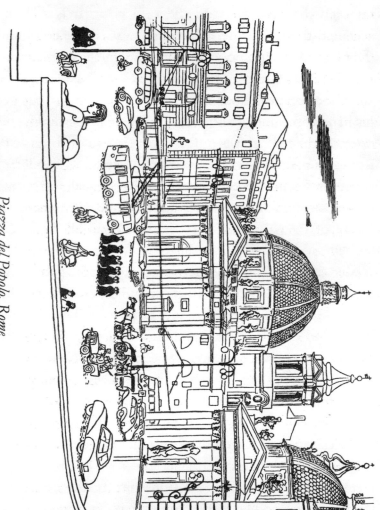

Piazza del Popolo, Rome

to in the newspapers as simply 'Ty' and 'Orson.' Frantic crowds gather round them if they appear in the pavement restaurants, even late at night.

It is just possible that the reason for all this is that, having abruptly lost Mussolini, and then their King, the Italians, being individualists, are hungry for someone to admire. The local politicians, though respected, have not as yet produced a really glamorous figure, and so the American stars stepped into an emotional gap.

There was a time when the Italian film industry itself used to be content to put out run-of-the-mill productions for local consumption, scoring an international *succès d'estime* here and there with such films as *To live in Peace* and *Bicycle Thieves*. It was the simplicity and naturalness of their best films, a sort of careless ad hoc quality – something that came out of the life of Italy itself – that probably gave them their special charm.

Now it looks as though everything is to be changed. The Italian companies themselves are bidding for Hollywood stars to come over for a month or two and play in films which are being specially written for the American market. The directors will be Italian, but the spoken dialogue will be English. The plots will be American. And so the de-Italianisation of Italy goes on.

But in all this I mean only to refer to the cities in Italy. In the country we found that 1949 came gently to its expected close and the New Year opened, according to schedule, with a series of political demonstrations and a crisis in the de Gasperi Cabinet. Yet there was one new thing, and again it had to do with the weather. Instead of a drought we got a continuous downpour of rain for 15 days and nights. In Tuscany the Arno ran over its banks and flooded Pisa. ('I have been expecting this,' Annunzio said, 'for a fortnight.') Up at Fiesole we live on terraces buttressed by very old stone walls, some of them dating back to Etruscan times. Towards the end of the first week of this exceptional rain the wet and loosened soil between the olive trees and the vineyards began to creep downhill. Little by little it put an intolerable pressure on the walls, so that each day as I walked down towards the Badia Fiesolana I noticed that the stones bulged outward a little more. Then cracks, big enough to put your hand into, developed; and we made the children walk cross-country to school rather than along the road. And still it rained. The first landslide occurred in the night. We heard nothing but a curious sighing noise, somewhere outside in the rain; almost a kind of gasp that went on for perhaps fifteen seconds. When I went down to the road in the morning I found that about twenty yards of wall, some ten feet in height, had crashed down, bringing with it two olive trees and a great river of mud. On my way home another part of the wall came down behind me with that same curious sigh.

After that these landslides occurred every night until we were cut off from the village, and whole acres of land which had been cultivated for the last two thousand years were lost to the peasants. The old stones seemed to tear like paper, and a lot of very ancient things were lost. The rain stopped of course, and at this moment the peasants are putting up new walls. But it is hard to get stone masons these days. Most of the young men want to get off the land and down to the city. You can get good wages as a waiter, plus tips, in the tourist season, and you are close to the movies there. And so many of the broken walls are just being left where they are. Probably there's a moral in this somewhere.

Chapter Six

Look, Signore!
Water Emerges!

The Italian Touring Club is still selling a pre-war guide-book which describes Cassino as a gay and vivacious little town on the banks of the river Rapido in Central Italy. It seems that the houses used to straggle picturesquely up the hillside close on top of one another; there were the remains of a Roman amphitheatre, a mediaeval fortress and a villa where Marc Anthony is supposed to have had orgies. The big day of the week was market day, on Saturday, and Mussolini had recently cleared the district of malaria.

Quite apart from the town and 1,500 feet directly above it stood the Benedictine monastery of Monte Cassino, a great oblong block of buildings that dominated the whole valley along the road to Rome, perhaps the most famous monastery in Europe.

This pleasant picture disintegrated on 8 September 1943, the day when Italy announced she had signed an Armistice with the Allies, and the day the first bombs fell on Cassino. Five months later, on the 15 February 1944, the monastery was destroyed in the most concentrated air attack which had yet been delivered in the war – an event which provoked almost as much debate at the time as the explosion of the first atomic bomb. A month later the town was wiped out.

In the five and a half years since then quite a lot of things have happened at Cassino. As there was practically nothing left of either the monastery or the town, both of them had to start rebuilding from scratch – not just the actual buildings, but the social and private lives of the communities as well – and so their story is probably a fair cross-section of what has been going on in one way and another in all the destroyed towns of Europe.

For the first few months while the war still rolled over the district, nothing was done; the monks dispersed, the inhabitants of Cassino wandered over the hills, many of them living like wild animals in caves and hovels, bearing children in the open, dressed in rags and grubbing up vegetable roots from the ground. Women sold their wedding rings to get food.

Then the plans for rebuilding began to develop. The problem of the monastery was fairly simple. Since it was unlikely that the twentieth century could produce anything better or even as good as the monumental architecture, the works of art, or the traditions of the preceding centuries, the Benedictines resolved that, as far as possible, everything should be restored to what it was before. Indeed the Abbot adopted the motto: *'Dov' era, com' era'* — 'Where it was and as it was.'

The position with the town below was just the reverse. For all its charm the old Cassino of 1943 was an uncomfortable and an insanitary place. It was perched awkwardly on the steep side of the hill, partly as a means of defence against marauding barons, and partly because there was so much malaria on the plains below. Drainage and DDT have killed the malarial mosquitoes and marauding barons have vanished for the time being. And so the authorities have adopted the motto 'Somewhere else and entirely different.' They have abandoned the ruins of the town, a cascade of grey rubble tumbling down towards the Rapido, and have begun rebuilding a completely new city on the plains.

It has always been like this at Cassino. When the Lombards destroyed the monastery in 558, and the Saracens again in 884, and even when an earthquake demolished the place in 1349, the monks patiently set to work each time to put things back more or less as they were before. But in Cassino town, which has been sacked by Hannibal, the Goths and Vandals as well as the Saracens, they change. At least once before this the town has been abandoned and rebuilt in another way in another place. In other words, the traditions stay the same up on the sacred mountain, but modern plumbing and modern ideas are adopted in the worldly plains below. Both communities seem to have found this an agreeable arrangement up to now; their only cry is that they should be left in peace. But Cassino is the classic battlefield of Italy, the place where nearly every army is baulked on its road to Rome. Nobody has really been able to relax around these parts for the last thousand years or so; but then men think they can and so they are hopefully rebuilding now for the next thousand years.

The rhythm of the work is interesting. The first thing they had to do was to clear away the debris left by the war and pick up the land mines. (Land mines are still being uncovered: a boy was blown to bits a week or two back). Next, they had to re-drain the marshes because water had collected in the bomb holes and mosquitoes were breeding again. Thirdly, the aqueduct had to be rebuilt to provide drinking water from the mountain springs. Fourth, they began on the houses and the hospital. But they had not gone far with this before they discovered that it is not comfort or health that apparently brings a community together, but law, or at any rate a visible demonstration of law.

The war had left the local people in a hopeless tangle. Half of them were living on someone else's property and refusing to get out. Ploughs and oxen and bedsteads and candlesticks had been borrowed and re-borrowed or sold or bartered or lost. And now where were the new property boundaries to be re-drawn after the rubble was cleared away? Who was to be compensated by what? And when and where and how much? The disputes were endless and embittered by utter poverty. So they were forced to put up a law court. And since a court needs a gaol if it is going to function, they went right on and built one – a very fine institution it is too, with accommodation for 120 now and 200 later on.

After this the construction of dwellings, roads, the city hall, the railroad station, the hospital and the schools went forward fairly evenly together. The last stage is the cinema and the new public gardens.

All this work has bounded ahead with staggering rapidity in the last few months. When you come into Cassino now on Highway Six, the road from Rome, the first impression is that of a south-west town that has suddenly struck oil. Some forty buildings are going up, and there is a roar of dynamiting around the Roman amphitheatre, where they are going to build an orphanage out of American funds, privately given. Electric lighting came on a few months ago and down the wide main street there is a train of brightly lit drug stores, restaurants and gas stations. Four hotels have sprung up, and since this is a convenient luncheon point midway between Rome and Naples, they catch the American tourists who have either just come off their boats at the beginning of their holiday or are about to start their voyage home.

On almost any day this year you would see a line of American, and British automobiles and buses drawn up along the main street among the white bullocks, the donkey carts and the women carrying bundles on their heads.

The tourists sat in the sunshine on the terraces paying astronomical prices for meals served in the grand hotel manner. And all around them spread the dusty air, the graveyards, the swarms of barefoot children, the sounds of blasting and hammering, the monastery up above and that queer grey patch of the mountain side where there is always a stray figure pottering among the ruins of old Cassino and occasionally sending a landslide of powdered rock on to the flats below.

There may still be things of value under the debris, a piece of jewellery or even perhaps a bit of furniture that has miraculously escaped. Occasionally they come on a skeleton, and if there is a scrap of clothing left, they can usually tell whether it is an Italian civilian, an Allied soldier or one of the German parachutists who put up such a fanatical defence on these slopes five and a half years ago. In the excavations for the new orphanage round the amphitheatre they have uncovered two Roman tombs, and bones were lying there among lamps and other household objects dating back nearly two thousand years. Indeed, as they cut down into the earth they are discovering relics of all the invaders who came here and stayed for a time. The amphitheatre itself (it was built by a Roman matron named Ummidia Quadratilla who was very fond of spectacles), has a bomb hole in the middle of it; but, like the Castle of Rocca Ianula up above, it survived the shock and simply became a little more ruined than it was before.

The real problem in the town, of course, is a social one, and it was taken on in the first years after the war by an institution which still survives under the name of UNRRA CASAS. Unrra Casas hunted round the surrounding villages and found many of the dispersed people of Cassino were running wild. They had lost touch with modern society. A whole generation of children were growing up who never washed, never changed their clothes either awake or asleep, and received no education at all. They were hungry, dirty, diseased and cold, and many of them had never been inside a proper house, let alone a hospital or a school. The overcrowding was ferocious. This is by no means a backward part of Italy, but it is no uncommon thing for the whole family to sleep fully clothed in one bed, and the families tend to run up to ten or more. There is very little machinery in the countryside. The fields are tilled with a wooden plough drawn by bullocks, and the grain is threshed by hand. In October you can see the vintner with his boots off crushing the grapes with his bare feet. The regional costume for the women is a wide black skirt, a white blouse with sleeves that are pleated sideways and a kerchief which is drawn over the head or the shoulders according to the weather. The poorer workers tend to wear pointed leather sandals which are laced up over thick white stockings that reach the knees. It is a great place for domestic animals and birds, especially turkeys. There is hardly a meadow where you do not see either a small child or an old man armed with a long stick minding a mixed bag of perhaps one pig, two sheep, a goat or a flock of turkeys or geese. There is no electric light or gas in most of the houses and no heating. Many neither read nor write. Women join the men in all the heavy work in the fields, and carry most of their burdens – a sack of wheat or a crate of chickens – on their heads. Permanent unemployment of anything up to 30 per cent or more is the usual thing.

These conditions were made much worse by the destruction of Cassino and the surrounding towns. Unrra first got a little food, clothing and medicine into the countryside and then started on the new houses. They chose a two-storey oblong design which consisted of four apartments, each of two bedrooms, a kitchen-living room, a tiny bathroom and an outside staircase, and the idea was that there should be no more than two people to a room or six to an apartment. The competition for these houses was naturally fierce, and even when the most desperate and deserving families were selected, there were unexpected complications. Unrra insisted that before getting possession the people must first take a shower-bath. Both men and women protested that it was immodest; they had never taken off their clothes before and they weren't going to start now. Moreover, they argued, they would catch cold and die of pneumonia. 'All right,' Unrra replied, 'no bath, no house.' This might have clinched the thing, but a new and fiercer protest came from the women, especially the young girls of marriageable age: their hair would get wet. In this part of Italy it is the custom of the women to do up their hair in two long plaits, and these are looped behind the head and pinned on top. Once the plaits are in position, there they stay – one might, of course, have to replait them occasionally as the years go by, but that is all. Unrra was now demanding the unthinkable – that the women should not only expose their heads to soap and water, but allow themselves to be seen in public with their hair falling down on their shoulders. Actually, once Unrra had had its way, things turned out rather well. The young girls emerged from the shower-baths to dry their hair in the sun and found the men looking at them with extraordinary interest: those waves of dark thick hair were something new in the village life. A vogue for cutting the hair and letting it go free has started in Cassino.

In the apartment itself, the chief wonder was the toilet with running water, for such an article had never been seen before. Going round some of the new settlements this week I found myself being constantly led up to the miraculous contraption in the bathroom: 'Look! Look carefully, signore. You pull this and *ecco*! Water emerges!' Most of my conversations were conducted against a background of constantly rushing water.

If a family keeps its apartment decently over a period of years, it will eventually be made the owner without payment. In the meantime, a rental of a dollar a month is charged, but no one as yet has had the heart to collect the money, for a dollar is six-hundred lire and six-hundred lire might be a day's food.

Though Unrra still keeps working, it has been outstripped now by two other organisations – European Recovery Programme and an Italian body, known as Genio Civile – and these have undertaken the main work of rehabilitation. Of Cassino's original 20,000 population, they have got back about 10,000 into the new town, and provided the money keeps coming the remaining 500 families will be installed, and the town completed about five years from now. The bulk of the money comes from the Italian government.

Just at this moment, when they are half way through the job, one comes upon weird contrasts in the town. The street lighting is some of the best in Italy, but I was only able to discover one telephone in the urban area, and that was in a shack behind the Post Office. A switchboard of a kind had been rigged up on a wooden bench, and beside it was an hour glass to gauge the time taken with each call. When, and if one got through to a number, the operator turned over this glass and the sand began to fall at the rate of one glassful a minute. They had a clock too, I noticed, but nobody seemed to trust it very much.

It's a little early yet to judge, but the chances are that the new Cassino will not be an ugly town. The piazza will be wide and long, and the blocks of apartments are being set at disparate angles to one another. Most of them are coloured different shades of ochre and sage and pale pink, which takes the barrack-like curse off them, and flower gardens are already being planted. But inevitably when everything is finished the place will look like an institution of some kind – perhaps a large hospital or a sanatorium. The majority of the people will live in precisely the same sort of apartments, sleeping in the same sort of beds and probably eating the same food off the same plates. Even the imitation wall-paper in the apartments is the same, for in these days of progress it is printed on the walls with a rubber roller. Indeed, this is the deliberate aim of the planners – to mass-produce, to get the people into houses as quickly, and cheaply, as possible. And, for the moment, the people are delighted with the idea. They are not asking for anything beautiful or attractive. As far as one can make out they don't want to be different from one another. One has only to visit some of the families who are still waiting for an apartment to realise why. There is a collection of them living in wooden shacks in a place called San Sylvestro which has grown up haphazardly between the new town and the old. The people here are barely clutching their way back towards civilised society as yet. They are at that worst stage of poverty, where all around them they can see the evidence of something better and still from month to month their lives drag on without gas or electric light or running water or even proper beds to sleep on.

In the old days they had a rough comfort, and there was a certain traditional rhythm in their lives. The average household was an overcrowded and insanitary affair, but it was cheerful, and to the lordly eye of the tourist, there was a great beauty in the terra-cotta cooking pots, the strings of tomatoes and onions hanging from the ceiling and the worn and solid furniture. Every house was different and had, as it were, a personality of its own. There was a flavour of simplicity and timelessness – that feeling of change in sameness that comes, like the cycle of the seasons, from things that have been done over and over again by many generations.

The new generation don't want terra-cotta cooking pots. They want aluminium. They want motor-cycles, strip lighting, telephones, and, possibly, tubular steel furniture. For the last few years the radio, the newspapers, the travellers from the big cities and the new advertisement hoardings, which are rapidly going up along Highway Six, have been pouring these new ideas in on them, so that now an urban way of life seems the only possible kind of progress. If it all ends in their living like robots in a kind of Huxleyan brave new world, well – *fa niente* – anything is better than this earthen floor and the rain and cold that pours through the cracks in the roof in the winter.

Later on, of course, things may change. I noticed that already one or two of the more successful business men and officials are putting up their own little villas of distinctive design and they are choosing sites, not on the plain, but back on the hillside again.

But in two important ways the whole character of the town is changing. To provide work the authorities have been compelled to turn Cassino into a manufacturing centre. A brewery and a bottling plant are going up. There is to be a factory for manufacturing spaghetti and other pasta (which once used to be hand-made every morning in every house by every wife). And still another plant is to make furniture and toys. Labour is cheap and abundant. Hops and wheat and timber will come from the surrounding hills. Each morning the workmen will step out of their municipal apartments, drop their children off at the municipal school and proceed just a few yards further on to the municipal assembly line. It is, I must repeat, a prospect that delights them.

The other new aspect is perhaps a little ominous. Cassino happens to be a famous name because a great battle was fought there, and a great monastery lies nearby. Many other towns round about were fearfully damaged too – but who (with the exception of the people of Glen Cove, Long Island, who have adopted the place) has heard of Pontecorvo, just 20 km away? Pontecorvo was smashed too, but Cassino gets the publicity. This is where the politicians come to make their speeches on the new Italy springing from its ruins. This new town is to be the show piece of the new democracy. Already, in 1949, foreign tourists arrived in great numbers – not only the devout and the curious, who climb those 1,000 feet up to the monastery, but the parents and relatives who want to see the graves of their sons and the country where they died. This year is Holy Year in Italy, and many thousands of pilgrims will be coming here. Inevitably, all this is turning Cassino from a poor town into a rich one, and even a slightly spoiled one. The more agile of the local people have leaped into the tourist trade with gusto. The restaurants and the gas-stations are already operating. Very soon the guides will appear along with the car park attendants, the stalls with picture postcards and souvenirs, the street beggars, the taxis, the slot machines, the coloured parasols and the flowers along the sidewalk and those little shops full of lace and hand-made baskets, which display a sign, saying '*English Spoken*,' '*Ici on parle Français*' Prices will fall in the winter, and then take an exultant bound upward with the spring. These things, no doubt, will coincide with the disappearance of the local costume, of the painted hand-carts, of pigs wandering down the main street, of the hour-glass in the telephone bureau and the endless idle gossip in the sunshine.

Just now it is in the transitional state. This Saturday, as always, the people streamed in from the surrounding country to the market and distributed themselves comfortably on the vacant allotments among the new and rising buildings – the terra-cotta pots and baskets in one place, the bellowing pigs and goats in another, the clothing stalls in the street running down to the railroad station and the chickens and turkeys just anywhere. Tourist buses and cars from Naples got hopelessly wedged in the crowd, and by ten o'clock there was a fearful hullabaloo round the church (now half rebuilt) when a family of black pigs got mixed up with a cart full of crucifixes, and a bull-dozer towing a load of cement. Each Saturday the country people find that another building is springing up on the vacant land where they used to sell their things

Exit from St. Peter's

and they have to move to a different place. Soon a market building will have to be built to cope with the situation. Later still, no doubt, the market itself will vanish. The stuff will go straight into the shops.

Clearly all this is going to change Cassino beyond recognition and clearly as far as material living conditions go, the new town will be better than the old one. Whether or not human nature is going to change with it is another matter. There is as yet no sign that the process of reducing a community to the direst extremity and then bringing it back to life and prosperity again is having any marked effect at all. The same political line-up exists – there was a swing to the Left directly after the war, but this is a conservative community of mildly royalist hue, and the communists now barely add up to 1 or 2 per cent. The same families who were successful before seem to be emerging again. The same faith, an implicit acceptance of Roman Catholicism, persists. There would appear to be the same proportion of villains, near villains, near saints and just ordinary people. The pursuit of money still governs a great part of life as it always did – it is only the horizons which are wider and the skill in getting money is greater.

I was told one revealing story. A little boy, the son of a bootmaker, broke his leg one night. The doctor took him to the new X-ray clinic, put the leg in plaster and dispensed some medicine. For these services the father produced all he had – his life savings of 20,000 lire. The clinic took it all and demanded more.

There are people agitating now to try and get a charity grant for the bootmaker, but no one as far as I could make out attached any blame to the doctor or the clinic. They were in business, like anybody else, they argued, and they were entitled to make what money they could. After all, these wonderful new gadgets like X-ray were a great luxury; in the old days, the boy might easily have remained a cripple. Life in Cassino is still just as hard as that.

On the other hand, I spent an hour with a carpenter named Pietro Rocco, a typical character, who was fairly bursting with the bustle and well-being that is beginning to pervade parts of Cassino now. His house was bombed to dust in 1943, he was forced into a German labour camp and he went through all the heavy bombardments of the town. One of his sons fought in Russia, and has never been heard of since, and another was a prisoner in Asmara. During these post-war years he, and the remains of his family, have lived in rags and hunger – until a few months ago. Now his trade booms, he has been moved into a new apartment, prices have started to come down, and at fifty his life begins to start again.

The apartment was beautifully clean.

'Thank God,' his wife cried, 'for America, who has made all this possible.'

'Ah, America.' Signor Rocco replied.

His pretty daughter ran to the toilet and pulled the chain. 'Look, Signore! Water emerges!'

They stood there, amid the sounds of the emptying cistern, as content a family group as you could hope to see.

One might argue, then, that Cassino is pursuing the normal course of any town that has struck it lucky and made a virtue of its calamity. But the monastery up on the mountain does add a special factor. Physically, it fills the eye, and in Cassino one is always conscious of it perching silently up there and suggesting another way of life entirely removed from gas stations and assembly lines.

It takes an hour and a half to walk up to the monastery, though formerly you could do it in a kind of ski-lift in seven minutes. Once there, the geographical importance of the place becomes immediately apparent. This is one of the spectacular panoramas of Europe. Monte Cairo rises higher still, much higher, on the slopes behind, and usually with a cloud about its summit at this time of the year. Down below the whole plain of the River Liri spreads out, the new Cassino directly below looks like a careless collection of children's toys flung down on the ground, and it is obvious that General Clark's army could never have passed this way without first taking the monastery. The peaks of the Abruzzi, one of the wildest parts of Italy, rise up to the south and just at sunset they turn strange colours of rose and lavender.

Somewhere about AD 525 St Benedict is believed to have come here upon a divine inspiration, having fasted for three years in a cave where a monk kept him alive by lowering bread to him in a basket. He demolished the Roman idol of Apollo on the mountain top and gave to his followers the famous rule, which has since become the basis of all western monasticism. It provides that in addition to the vows of poverty, chastity and obedience, the monks are obliged to acquire knowledge and engage in manual work. In the one thousand four hundred years since then the chief fame of the monastery is that it has been one of the few little lights of learning that have always burned in Europe, and there were times when it had great wealth and influence. The library alone, with its twenty thousand volumes, was a great treasure, and to this was added a private library of forty thousand volumes, musical archives and rare prints. Last century a meteorological and geodynamic observatory was put up and the monastery's recordings of earthquakes was the oldest in the world.

After so many rebuildings, Monte Cassino was perhaps nothing very great architecturally. But it was a massive place conceived as a town, a rectangle of stone 198 metres long and 140 broad. Its doors were open to anyone who wished to study, and guest houses, a hospital and a school were enclosed in the huge building. Both Luca Giordano and Bassano painted frescoes here and the choir stalls in the Basilica were regarded as one of the treasures of Italy. The hillsides round about were covered with groves of olives, cypresses, oak, ilex and pine.

Up to the time of the war some sixty monks were working here under the abbot, and as the headquarters of the Benedictines the place was one of the principal shrines of Christianity.

Then on 15 February came the bombing; and this is a matter that has been be-devilled by a controversy ever since. One of the first things you notice at Cassino is that, sooner or later, everyone slips a reference to it into the conversation. 'Of course,' they say, 'there were no Germans in the monastery at the time.' There may have been Germans on the slopes below the walls, they add, but none actually inside the monastery itself.

The Allied Command at the time declared that the Germans were inside the buildings, and after a good deal of public discussion announced their intention of destroying them.

In the light of the evidence that has come up since then the Allied case seems rather weak. It could hardly be argued that the monastery was destroyed because it was a German observation post, because there were plenty of other observation posts on the mountain side which were just as good – anyway, you don't destroy an observation post like this by bombing: you have to knock the whole mountain down. Nor do you destroy a defensive position by demolishing a building – the defenders can, and in fact did, fight just as well, or even better, in the rubble which makes a bomb-proof ceiling for the cellars. No German guns were seen to fire from the building up to the time of the bombing, though they did take up positions there *afterwards*, and, indeed the Germans claim the whole operation was more favourable to them than to us.

The monks are now selling a postcard which is a photograph of a drawing made in the monastery by a German soldier at the time. It shows a villainous Churchill leading a string of bombers up from the plains below, while a handsome young German parachutist stands on the ruins of the monastery above. He is saying, complacently, 'Well, fancy that!' To some people, especially those whose sons died here trying to get the Germans out of Italy, the selling of this postcard might seem in rather poor taste, but it gives an indication of how deeply the monks feel about the subject.

Probably the whole laborious dispute might best be ended by it being admitted that the bombing was a desperate act at the height of a desperate battle when *everything* had to be tried to gain the larger object of the victory; and certainly it is true that the Germans *could* have occupied the monastery at any moment they chose.

At all events there are some facts that nobody disputes: when the Allied armies first came up to the position, a quantity of books, religious ornaments, and some of the pictures were evacuated to Rome for safe-keeping. Only a handful of monks remained behind with the Abbot. When the bombardment of Cassino town grew bad a party of terrified women came to the monastery and threatened to set fire to the building, unless the doors were opened. The doors were opened, and about a thousand Italian civilians came in. With the battle raging all round them and supplies cut off, they lived a frightful existence underground, and many of them were killed when the bombs came down on 15 February.

The raid started at 9 a.m. and continued for five hours. According to General Maitland Wilson's report to the combined Chiefs of Staff, 142 Fortress bombers dropped 287 tons of 500 lb. general purpose bombs, and 66½ tons of 100 lb. incendiaries, followed by 47 B. 25's and 40 B. 26's, which dropped another 100 tons of high explosive bombs.

Not all these bombs found the target since some of them fell on the French Headquarters at Venafro, miles away; but that last 100 tons seems to have settled the matter. The huge stone walls were observed to sag and then collapse in upon themselves, and a vast column of smoke climbed up above Monte Cairo. Subsequent bombings completed the destruction and the surrounding forests were so devastated that to-day one sees little but bare rock.

Those monks and civilians who survived evacuated the place after the raid, (though one brother aged 90 lingered on for six weeks until he died), and the German parachutists took possession of the ruins. Among the wreckage was almost all the private library.

The motto of Monte Cassino is *Succisa Virescit*, and there is a tradition that it always rises again. Among the monks themselves there are architects, engineers, builders and experts in sculpture and painting, and they still possess the plans of the building as it was. Their first job was not only to clear the debris away, but to pick out of it every morsel of stone or metal or woodwork that possibly could be pieced together again. Apart from some of the cellars, only the crypt of the Basilica, a late construction with a curious Egyptian decoration, was left wholly intact, and, miraculously, the tomb of St Benedict himself. Around these two points the rebuilding began.

To-day, as you come up to the entrance to the monastery, you find all that corner of the building has been restored, and over the front door there has been boldly painted the word PAX. Beyond it to the right, through many vaulted cloisters, the refectory has been entirely rebuilt, a large oblong hall now filled with an exhibition of plans, photographs and models, which show how the monastery is being put together again. Further on, the basilica which was begun only four months ago, is half finished. One sees beside St Benedict's tomb there the crater where an unexploded bomb fell. In the court-yard outside, some two hundred men are working under the direction of the monks among a network of railway lines, fallen pillars and decapitated statues. By groping about in the rubble they have rescued statues and slabs of inlaid marble, which were broken into as many as 50 pieces. A kind of jig-saw game goes on – a business of fitting marble arms and fingers and noses to the right places; and when the craftsman finds that a piece is irrevocably lost he carves it again himself and sticks it on. He is bound by the instruction 'Where it was and as it was,' and the work will go on for years. One of the few parts of Giordano's frescoes left is a small stone medallion showing a head of St Benedict weeping.

Outside the walls the Abbot, Monsignore Rea, has built a temporary house for himself and thirty of the monks who have come back to supervise the work and revive the Benedictine school again. Below the monastery the bare slopes have been re-terraced and planted with olives and other trees. Soon the library will be rebuilt and there will be returned to it the manuscripts and the thirty thousand books, which are in safe-keeping at Rome. But this is a major part of the reconstruction and progress depends a good deal on finance. It is a condition of ERP that money cannot be spent upon religious institutions, and so the Benedictines have had to rely upon church and Italian government funds, upon donations from pilgrims coming here and upon private collections throughout the world. They have received up to now $6,000 from America. Perhaps 30 per cent of the major work has already been done, though the finer things, like the rich decoration of the basilica, are, of course, irreplaceable.

It was the Poles who took Monte Cassino in the end, and over a thousand of them now lie in a fold in the hills beneath the monastery. The Americans who fought here have been gathered in another place not far away. At the foot of the mountain four thousand British are lying – British, Indians, New Zealanders, and half a dozen other nationalities who struggled here for six hard months before they won. Quite a few of the soldiers have never been identified, and so one reads on the tombstone simply 'Known unto God.'

Between these cemeteries and the noisy forward-looking town below and the monastery up above, with its life fixed in the past, one gets a revealing glimpse of history going by. And despite the waste, and all the depressing evidence of the past, there is something hopeful about it all, or at any rate rather re-assuring.

Chapter Seven

To Keep the Infidel at Bay

Since the bootleg days, when Al Capone and half a dozen other gangsters first migrated to America, Sicily seems to have had a reputation for breeding bandits. They lie dormant for a while, then, like Etna and the other volcanoes off the coast, they suddenly erupt. It reminds one a good deal of Ireland (which has about the same size and population as Sicily) in the old days of rebellion against England.

Like the Irish, the Sicilians are temperamentally against government, or at any rate government imposed from outside the island. The local boy who breaks the law expresses something of everybody's dislike of the police, especially if they are foreign police. And so there was a good deal of sympathy here for the young man known as

Salvatore Giuliano, who was the latest operator in the Al Capone tradition.

Since Giuliano has been engaged in continuous brigandage for the past six years or more and is credited with having murdered, or caused to be murdered, upwards of two hundred people beside holding up dozens of Sicilian aristocrats and business men to ransom, it has become a little difficult to separate him from the myth that has naturally gathered round his name.

A Swedish woman journalist who succeeded in reaching one of Giuliano's hiding places, was enraptured with him. On the other hand, an Italian police chief named Signor Pappalardo described him as 'a delinquent, pitiless thug, who gives no mercy and asks for none.' More recently Colonel Luca, who is currently in charge of the operations against bandits, spoke of Giuliano as 'a crazy megalomaniac.' One of Giuliano's kidnap victims, who spent some days with him waiting for his ransom to be paid, said he had a 'rather distinguished and courteous manner.' They ate macaroni and tomatoes and talked about astronomy.

Certainly the photographs of Giuliano taken about the time he began his career are disarming. They show a round good-tempered face, much burnt by the sun, a high forehead, a large mouth, a solidly built figure with a suggestion of the out-of-doors in the way he holds himself and very strong, wide hands. He has a refreshing smile and in most of the pictures there is a horse hanging about somewhere.

His letters – and he writes frequently to the Sicilian newspapers, politicians, his prospective victims and anyone who takes his fancy – reveal a moderately good handwriting, a little sprawling, but direct and confident. I saw the latest of these letters written on plain notepaper to a Sicilian merchant. 'Illustrious Sir,' it begins, 'if you value your life you will pay me fifty million lire.' There are some terse instructions: a car with a basket on the roof covered with a white cloth must proceed along a certain road until it is stopped by a man who will ask the driver if he is coming from Rome. Then the money must be paid over in bank-notes. If not – death. The victims usually pay.

All those who have seen Giuliano agree upon his sobriety and simplicity. He eats plain country meals, mostly vegetables, pasta and fruit, and rarely, if ever, touches hard liquor. He has very little interest in women, and he is said to have taken fierce disciplinary action against any debauchery among his men.

Various picturesque stories are told of his special brand of courtesy with women. Once, for example, he entered the room of a Sicilian duchess and asked for her jewels. She pleaded that at least she should keep her engagement ring, because it had a sentimental value. 'Then I shall value it all the more,' Giuliano is supposed to have said – and took the ring.

On another occasion, when he blocked the Palermo-Trapani rail-road by putting an obstacle across the line, his men rode alongside on horseback and commanded all the male passengers to descend and lie face downwards on the ground, so that their pockets could be rifled. The women were allowed to remain in their seats while they were robbed.

With the poor Giuliano is supposed to have a lavish hand, distributing 10,000 lire notes to those who bring him food. He protested in a letter to a local newspaper that at 50 million lire, his ransom fee was not large, considering the increasing difficulty of the work and the number of poor peasants he had to maintain. Once he arrested a poor man by mistake; the man was released at once, merely being asked to pay his board and lodging. At Christmas Giuliano presented gifts of food to the orphanages round Palermo, and he has been known to send wreaths to the funerals of his victims. He has, too, a certain ruthless sense of humour. When Signor Scelba, the Italian Minister for the Interior (incidentally another Sicilian), put a price of several million lire on his head, Giuliano retaliated by offering an even higher sum for Signor Scelba, dead or alive.

These sort of stories – and there are scores of them – have caused a formidable legend to grow up. It is the picture of a poor country boy like any other Sicilian, who got in wrong with the police, one thing led to another, and now, because of the rottenness of post-war politics, he finds himself a major criminal.

There may be some truth in all this, but one needs to know something about the peculiarities of life in Sicily to sort it out. Indeed, once you start going into Giuliano's career, you find yourself getting involved with the story of the whole island; and Giuliano begins to emerge more as an expression of a state of mind than an actual human being. The underlying principle seems to be that no community ever feels safe or at ease with itself until it begins to persecute someone else. Thus (to quote the supporters of this idea) the pilgrim fathers never felt really secure in America until they started driving back the red Indians. Similarly, in our time, the Jews in Israel only began to form a coherent state when they had demolished the Arabs. The Sicilians, on the other hand, have never had a chance to oppress anybody. They have always been poor and always occupied by somebody or other beginning with the Greeks in the eighth century BC and ending with the Italians in 1950.

Consequently, they are automatically against the government and more particularly the police. They claim that in the end all foreign governments are unjust and cruel and so, as a means of self-protection, they formed their own underground government, which is known as the Mafia. According to how you look at it the Mafia is either a conspiracy of the Ku Klux Klan variety or a patriotic brotherhood. There are no party meetings, no officials, no elections and no clear rules. It is simply an arrangement by which the strongest and sometimes the ablest men in every village take charge of the communal life and enforce their own kind of justice. They make threats, they extort money, they protect people from the police and other outside interference; and if necessary, they kill.

Before the war the Mafia was so strong in Sicily that Mussolini sent 30,000 men under the command of a General Mori, to stamp it out. 'Fascism,' he said, 'was quite good enough; there is no need for the Mafia any more.' There is a horrible warning to dictators in the story of how Il Duce launched his campaign in Sicily. It seems that a great crowd of Sicilians were gathered to welcome him, and one of the leading politicians of the island opened the proceedings with an impassioned denunciation of the Mafia. This pleased the Sicilians a good deal, for they all knew something that only Mussolini did not know – and this was that the speaker himself was the top man in the Mafia. However, by the outbreak of the war the Mafia *was* stamped out – but not the Mafia mentality. When the Allies landed in the summer of 1943, it sprang right back into action again.

This was where Giuliano entered the picture. He was just 22 at the time of the landings and he had had a career that might have happened to any other peasant's son. He left school very young to help on his parents' plot of land near Montelepre, a little village in the bare hills behind Palermo, about half an hour's drive from the town. The family was abjectly poor and after a bit Giuliano struck out on a job of his own – he bought olive oil in one place and sold it at a slightly better price somewhere else. After this he got a job as a linesman with a telephone company that was running a new line through Montelepre. At the time of the landings he was back at his oil selling again. He

Tuscan Landscape

had no criminal record and there was nothing particularly remarkable about him except his rather quick temper and his frank good looks.

With the arrival of the Allied armies, the value of the Italian lire collapsed, and Giuliano was not making enough money to keep alive. Like thousands of other Sicilians at that time of near starvation he began to do a little black-marketing on the side. Corruption was the usual thing in Sicily then, and it worked best for people who operated on a big scale, especially with a vital commodity like wheat. The small operator was apt to be picked up by the police, and one day Giuliano *was* picked up carrying a bag of grain on his horse. Now the police knew and Giuliano knew that everyone was dealing in grain – even the police themselves. And so in a wild outburst of indignation, he drew a gun and shot a *carabiniere* dead.

Presumably something happens in the mind of a man when he first commits murder. He either runs away or is so appalled that he surrenders, or he is seized with a kind of reckless desperation that makes him go on and murder someone else. At all events his character probably changes. Unfortunately – or perhaps fortunately – the Italians are an uninhibited people and they have very little interest in psychology. Nobody has yet bothered to find out exactly what happened to Giuliano during those first few months after his first killing. He simply took to the hills and – as one sees from his later letters – he nursed a feeling that was something between bragadoccio and deep resentment. It almost seems that he had the guilty feeling of the child who knows he has done something atrociously wrong and at the same time his pride and fear prevent him from confessing and accepting the consequences. Then, too, he had been lightly wounded in his scuffle with the police and this must have added to his bitterness. The villagers of Montelepre naturally sided with him in a body, and no doubt kept him supplied with food. Why, they argued, should Giuliano have been singled out when he had done nothing worse than anybody else? The killing, they said, was an accident.

During those early days while the war was still on, the Italian police were far too weak and disorganised to maintain an effective man-hunt and many nights, no doubt, Giuliano slept in his own bed at home. Through the winter of 1943–44 conditions were still ruinously bad for the Sicilians and the black market in looted US army stores and other goods developed into a settled routine. What had formerly been lawless now became the accepted way of life. Army weapons and ammunition were easily picked up, and for a desperate young man already wanted by the police, the temptations to take to banditry were very strong indeed.

Somewhere about this time a young Sicilian, who may have been Giuliano, entered a bank in Palermo, calmly snatched a bundle of the new Allied bank-notes off the counter and escaped. A little later – in January, 1944 – there was a gaolbreak at Monreale near Palermo. Ten prisoners, among them Giuliano's uncle and cousin, and a noted desperado named Tommaso di Maggio, got away. It was not long after this that killings and hold-ups around Palermo began to increase. By the end of the war it was apparent that the more desperate of the bandits were forming themselves into groups and the most successful of these groups was led by Giuliano.

Meanwhile, what was happening to the individual, Giuliano, was going on in a milder but much larger way all over Sicily. Released from Fascism and assured by the Allies that the new era of freedom had started, the Mafia began to re-appear in every village. Often UNRRA supplies, as well as local products, were parcelled out according to Mafia orders and it was sometimes difficult for a man to hold or get a job without the blessing of the Mafia. The only restraining influence was the presence of American and British Angot officers who could hardly hope to do much more than skate about the surface of these labyrinthine politics. At this time, too, the Allies were giving a certain amount of support (which was afterwards hastily withdrawn) to the movement to set up Sicily as an independent state, apart from Italy. Bandits, Mafia and politicians all jumped on this band-wagon with a will. Everyone, it seemed, right down to outright murderers, was acting for the good of Sicily.

The chances are that Giuliano really did feel that he had some kind of a mission at this time. He loathed the communists; on one occasion he ambushed one of their meetings in the hills, cold-bloodedly opened fire on the crowd and killed half a dozen or more. He flirted with the Separatist movement for a while, until they found his methods too drastic and dropped him. Then his men began plastering the walls of Palermo with slogans. 'Let the people vote,' Giuliano cried. 'Let them decide between me and the government. If I am defeated, I will give myself up.'

It was that same mixture of nihilism and violent righteousness that overtook many of the disbanded partisan groups in Northern Italy and France in the first few years after the war. For a long time these boys could not get used to the dull routine of peace. But, whereas in the north, many of the former partisans turned into communists or new fascists, there was a special flavour to the movement in Sicily. Like the Irish in Eire and the Jews in Israel, the Sicilians simply wanted the right to govern themselves.

The Sicilian is very different to the Italians in the north. He is a mixture of Greek, Arab, Norman and Spanish, as well as a native Italian. He is less vivacious than the Neapolitans, less subtle than the Romans or the Florentines, and less practical than the Milanese. He has a hard core of pride. An insult which is lightly flung across the street in Naples would start a vendetta here in Palermo. Many times as a boy Giuliano must have seen the puppet shows in Palermo, which are one of the most charming things in the island. These shows are nearly all based on Charlemagne and the Carolingian legends: the Christian knights are dressed in shining armour, they are all incredibly noble and brave, and they fall upon the Saracens and the infidels (i.e., the invaders) against the most desperate odds. A seat at these shows costs 20 lire and the legends they depict are so long that there is enough material to put on a different performance every night for 13 months. Scenes from the same legends appear on the famous painted carts of the peasants all over the island. Most Sicilian little boys grow up with an heroic vision of themselves as knights in shining armour. The nearest thing you get to such a character in modern Sicily is the glamorised bandit, the murderer, like Giuliano, who sends gifts to the convents and declares that he lives only for the liberation of his country.

By 1948 Giuliano was openly boasting that he controlled all the hills behind Palermo. 'How can they call me an outlaw,' he demanded, 'when the command of the island is mine?' He was fighting, he added, 'for Sicily.' Since Sicily had already been granted regional government by now, this war cry was a good deal less effective than it had been before. Moreover Giuliano's methods had less of the air of a crusade about them. To raise money he began kidnapping in a big way. There was nothing very subtle in his approach. The case of Signor Agnello, one of Palermo's leading merchants, was fairly typical.

Signor Agnello was taking his after-luncheon stroll through the city, when a black Fiat car drew up alongside him, a masked man jumped out and ordered him to get in. Signor Agnello demurred, but two more men set on him and after a brief struggle, he was flung into the back of the car and blindfolded. They travelled for about an hour when the car was abandoned, and after a long walk through the hills Signor Agnello found himself in a cave with Giuliano.

For the next two weeks he was taken from one cave to another, eating the simplest meals of vegetables and pasta, until eventually his family paid 50 million lire, and he was released.

In a similar way Giuliano has kidnapped an astonishing number of local princes, dukes, industrialists, officials and even members of the Chamber of Deputies. His ransom fee fluctuates between 30 and 50 million lire. In addition to this, he has exacted regular monthly blackmail fees from business houses and individuals in Palermo, levied a toll on the buses which pass through his territory (which is said to have extended over one tenth of the island), besides holding up occasional trains and automobiles. These operations have caused the deaths of nearly one hundred *carabinieri* and police agents and as many civilians. The exact figure will never be known, because there are people still missing, and it is never precisely certain whether certain killings were carried out by Giuliano and his men or some other gang.

Already little jackals have emerged and exacted money from people in Palermo by pretending to be representatives of Giuliano. Those who are apt to romance over Giuliano – and he has received many ecstatic letters from women

— sometimes forget that most of these killings were calculated acts of murder, usually planned beforehand and quite deliberately committed. A man in Montelepre who openly complained one day, 'How long is this going to go on? Why don't they catch him?' was found dead a few hours later.

By the summer of last year the authorities were getting pretty desperate about Giuliano. One of the powers conferred on the new Sicilian regional government was the right of keeping order on the island, but they were finding Giuliano too hot to handle. Mistakenly, perhaps, the police arrested Giuliano's mother on the grounds that she had erected a new house in Montelepre and could not explain where she got the money from. This really enraged Giuliano. He wrote to all the deputies demanding his mother's release. He wrote to the President of the Italian Republic and the newspapers. He sent a letter to President Truman, asking that he should be supplied with tanks, as part of Marshall Aid, so that he could conquer Sicily and declare it the forty-ninth state of the Union. To the Palermo government he threatened 'total war' – and as an earnest of this he made a point blank assault on a police station and killed a few more *carabinieri*.

A new element of ruthlessness enters into Giuliano's attacks from the time of his mother's arrest; it marked the stage of his turning from a minor outlaw with a half-realised schoolboy ambition, into a major killer who kills for the sake of killing. Some of his lieutenants, notably a certain

Cucinella, were monstrously cruel – capable of skinning an animal alive for amusement, capable even of dragging a wounded policeman behind a truck until he died. Once, when the *carabinieri* over-ran one of the bandit's camps they found that a dog had been nailed up inside a guitar so that it howled in terror whenever a string was plucked. Giuliano himself has never been charged with these sort of excesses: the police regard him as the practical and concentrated murderer who is never frivolous and who always acts with a purpose.

Not unnaturally by last year there was great fear in Palermo. Being human the majority of the people were not seriously upset over seeing a successful business man mulcted of a few millions: but for the business men themselves it was a deadly serious matter. No man when threatened dared go to the police. Some of them preferred to leave for Switzerland and only returned after their agents had made a deal with Giuliano. Once the police made a successful raid and recovered five million lire from one of the bandits. But when they took the money back to the man who had been blackmailed for it he refused to accept it, saying that he did not dare so long as Giuliano was at liberty. Equally the countryside around Palermo was intimidated. Often Giuliano announced in advance to a farmer that he intended to spend a night in his house. The farmer stocked up with provisions, left a 10,000 lire note on his mantelpiece, and decamped for the night with his family.

Finally last year, the central government in Rome sent to Palermo a force of 2,000 men, mostly bachelors and mostly non-Sicilians, and they were armed with tear gas, radio, reconnaissance planes, machine guns and armoured cars. At the head of this force was a Colonel Luca, an old guerrilla leader, whose career goes back to the days when he worked with Lawrence of Arabia in the Near East. Colonel Luca is a brisk and volatile Venetian in his early fifties, a short thick-set figure with slightly bulging eyes and a determined manner. He deployed at once for a considerable military campaign, and the third and probably the last phase of Giuliano's career began.

At first things went badly. Giuliano accepted the arrival of the new forces with defiance: he staged an all-out attack on the police barracks at Bellolampo, which means Beautiful Lightning. A truck load of Luca's men rushing to the scene were blown up by a land mine and seven were killed. Then the serious war of attrition began. Palermo was put under semi-military law and Montelepre was occupied. Visiting Montelepre now, one finds it powerfully reminiscent of the village scenes in Sicily during the Allied invasion. A cheerful character by the name of Major Levet Fetre has established his headquarters in a barber's shop in the main street and here is all the usual panoply of sentries, radios set up beside the camp beds, rifles and machine guns stacked against the wall, and military vehicles waiting outside. The surrounding hills are remarkably like those in parts of Palestine, bare, rocky, precipitous and filled with innumerable caves which have long been used as hide-outs for the bandits and tombs for the men they kill. One by one these caves are filled with heavy gas. The *carabinieri* go out on foot in patrols of ten, carrying radio sets. At night aircraft stand ready to drop parachutists and flares. In Montelepre itself, the Giuliano house, a smart two storey affair, on the edge of the village, has been locked up, but as you pass down the main street his relatives and friends greet you with that same kind of friendly but ironic reserve they had in the war. For them these *carabiniere*, in their thick boots and British style battle-dress, are foreigners: a point which a Sicilian military chaplain made clear enough when the new troops first arrived.

'Dear boys,' the Chaplain began, as he addressed them after an open-air mass, 'you are here in Sicily on these barren hills in touch with danger and ambush. In order that your task may be easier I must at once tell you an unpleasant truth: you are hated. The people in the villages do not consider you as protectors, but as pitiless executors of laws which do not originate in the island. Your arrival in the towns will not be greeted as a liberation, but as a cause for mourning: wherever you go hundreds of people will be detained, arrested, searched, sent to gaol. And should you arrest ten persons in a town you may be sure that you have struck the whole town. Here we are all something more than blood relations…'

Though strong and, perhaps tactless, there was no doubt a good deal of truth in this. A group of villagers dressed in black were standing nearby listening to the address, and by the way they exchanged glances and winked at one another, it was fairly clear that they agreed with the Chaplain. Above all Giuliano is Sicilian – that probably is the governing thing, for the Sicilians. He is protected by the code of *omertà*. This is the local tradition that no Sicilian will ever inform upon another, no matter what has happened. It is the basic loyalty, the one that is acknowledged before all others on the island. If a thief runs down the street you can turn to any passer-by and say: 'Which way did he go?': and the man will always shrug his shoulders and reply: 'I saw nothing.' From the first then, Colonel Luca has had to work with no information whatever, except what his own men collect themselves. Although Giuliano is known to be close to Montelepre at this moment every villager swears he has never seen him nor does he know anything about him. Quite apart from this *omertà*, most of the local people are afraid to speak.

No doubt when Giuliano is finally taken there will be a certain relief, mixed with the regret. But if you ask a Sicilian about his feelings now, he will say: 'If he is captured or killed – then that's all right. If not – well that's all right too'.

Within a month or so of Colonel Luca's arrival things began to change. Little by little through the fall last year his soldiers began to close in on the known hide-outs of the bandits. As it so often happens, they pulled in the smaller fry at first. Tommaso di Maggio, known as Uncle Masi, the man who escaped in the original gaolbreak in 1944, was taken in Montelepre itself. A character known as Salvatore Ferreri, or Brother Devil, was killed in action and Giuseppe di Lorenzo, the guitar player, was captured along with another man, Salvatore Speciale, who was surprised with his mistress in Messina at the other end of the island. Most of these arrests were made after gun battles, in one of which Giuliano himself is supposed to have been wounded again. Then the police made a really big coup when they picked up Guiseppe Cuccinella, one of Giuliano's chief aides, in a flat in Palermo. Cuccinella lost a leg when a hand grenade exploded. Ten times the normal amount of penicillin was pumped into him and he survived. He had three million lire with him when he was taken to hospital. By December last year arrests were occurring every week and the initiative had passed out of Giuliano's hands. Several of his men were captured while they were waiting to get aboard ships for America and it was estimated that of the original band of fifty or more very few remained.

There was a time when, if a morning newspaper in Palermo published a story about Giuliano, the editor received a reply from Giuliano himself the same afternoon, and often in an envelope stamped in Palermo. Now no more letters arrive. Deputies meeting at Sicily's regional parliament no longer receive visits from Giuliano's representatives instructing them how to vote.

All this makes things rather more difficult for Colonel Luca, for he is striking now into a void – or as he describes it, 'a conspiracy of silence' – whereas previously when the bandits were active, he had something definite to react to. I asked him if he himself had ever received a communication from Giuliano. 'Just menaces,' the Colonel said. But conditions are not quiescent just yet. During the ten days I have been here one *carabiniere* has been killed, a bomb has been thrown at a police station, three bodies have been recovered from a cave, at least one industrialist has been threatened with his life, and two country buses have been held up at machine-gun point. The incident of the cave was particularly horrible as the three bodies had been thrown down there 18 months previously. The first *carabiniere* who was lowered into the darkness on a rope nearly a hundred feet long collapsed when he was brought to the surface. Another *carabiniere* volunteered to go down with a gas mask and eventually the bodies were recovered. One gets an idea of the toughness of the bandits from an arrest that was made last year – one of them was found hiding in a thirty foot dry well where he had been for five days without food or water lying on the bodies of two men he had murdered.

There was one other incident last month. Luca's men got word that a ship illegally taking emigrants to Philadelphia was due to appear one night off the Sicilian coast to pick up 50 passengers. The ship never appeared and the *carabiniere* arrested the 50 people who had been waiting hopefully off the shore as they stepped from their fishing boats. Most of them were poor farmers who had sold up everything in order to get to America. They complained that the bandits had made life impossible in Sicily. Among them were five of Giuliano's men. Another batch of minor gangsters was arrested when the ship put into Sardinia a day or two later. Obviously then, an exodus has begun, and the end of the Giuliano gang is in sight.

But Giuliano himself is still here and the way the police look at it he will not try to go away. This deadly game has gone on so long now that there is a certain pride involved on both sides: to surrender has become the unthinkable thing. Giuliano has a great deal of money. No Sicilian – not even the Mafia, who have grown to detest him, because of the brigades of police and soldiers he has brought into Sicily – will give him away. There is no death penalty in Italy and Giuliano has been sentenced in *absentia* to something like a thousand years imprisonment – but this has ceased to be a serious consideration. It is the gestures which count now, the theatricality and the *amour propre* with which the last scenes are played out. The last word from Giuliano was that he is waiting patiently for the news that his mother has been released from prison; he has refrained, he says, on account of this from murdering Colonel Luca for the time being. He adds, somewhat enigmatically, that he is bound to win this contest in the end, because he is completely disinterested in his own life.

Last month three Italian journalists managed to see Giuliano at one of his hide-outs in the hills. The photographs they brought back reveal an overwhelming change. In place of the slightly happy-go-lucky air of five years ago Giuliano is revealed now with a heavy and brutish face. There is a certain slyness in the eyes, and he has grown much fatter and coarser. It is the face of the wary thug – and rather a minor thug at that. Looking at these pictures it seems hard to imagine that he was ever taken for a serious political figure. Of the famous air of courtesy and chivalry nothing remains except his sentimental and angry demands for his mother's release. Clearly the legend of the gentleman bandit parted company from the facts some time ago.

It is just possible that Giuliano has hopes that his own minor enormities might be overlooked in the major enormity of another war. In any event, a final gun battle, probably somewhere in Palermo itself, or more dramatically at Giuliano's birthplace at Montelepre, seems the most likely outcome, and the people of Palermo pick up their newspapers each morning with a certain fascinated detachment. Whatever happens they feel certain that Giuliano will not make a *brutta figura* – a poor showing – at the end. He will, they think, be defeated in action against the invaders.

Meanwhile, it is only fair to say that just a small part of Sicily has been affected by these doings. Life in towns like Messina, Catania and Palermo, goes by in a perfectly normal way. The shops are riding on a post-war business boom. The four and a half million population of the island keeps rocketing up at the rate of forty thousand a year, and nobody but a very small handful of people goes in fear of death or kidnapping.

Anyone planning a trip to Sicily this year can proceed with confidence. The early spring or the autumn is the best time, for then the Tyrrhenian Sea is a marvellous warm blue, the island glows with wild flowers and the air is scented by the almond groves and the bananas. The visitor should certainly not miss the puppet shows. He will find there dozens of Sicilian children looking much the same as Giuliano used to look as a small boy; and he will hear them roaring with excitement as Roland, the Christian Knight, comes marching on to the stage to keep the foreigners and the infidels at bay.

Giuliano was trapped in the hills near Palermo by Colonel Luca's men early in July 1950. They shot him dead.

Chapter Eight

The Ghost in the Villa

I

The Villa Bruscoli, or as it is now called, the Villa Diana, lies in a ravine about halfway down the steep slope of Fiesole on the cool, north-western side. It is a pleasant house, but the surroundings are strange and even harsh for Tuscany. Directly below the garden the land falls sharply down to the Mugnone River and then rises even more abruptly on the other side, so that the general outlook of the house is upon a wall of brown rocks and overhanging boulders.

In the winter the wind comes tearing along this valley from the north with an iciness and a persistence beyond anything you would expect in Italy; in the summer this is almost the last house on Fiesole to get the sun in the morning and the first to lose it in the evening.

The Villa itself is approached by a fine sweep of stone steps, very broad and shallow, with two small lions at the bottom standing rampant with their shields. Once you reach the top flight it is possible to look out either end of the ravine, and this is the more re-assuring view. To the north the valley breaks out into gentle Tuscan hills towards Cafaggiolo, which was one of the Medici's summer palaces in the fifteenth and sixteenth centuries. To the south one looks down on Florence with Brunelleschi's great brick-red dome rising from the cathedral in the centre. To the east, hidden by cypress groves and the curve of the hill, stands the Villa Medici on Fiesole; and Careggi, still another seat of the family, lies in the valley just over the other side of the ravine.

Everything about the countryside is old and it was already old when the Villa Diana was built five hundred years ago or more. These paths were made and these terraces were cultivated in just this way before the Romans arrived, perhaps even before Fiesole was a great Etruscan city in the third century BC and Florence was nothing. It is, in fact, one of the oldest inhabited places in Europe.

Above the front door of the Villa Diana a stone plaque has been let into the honey-coloured facade. It says in Italian:

In this house from 1483 to 1494 lived Agnolo Ambrogini called Poliziano the greatest humanist of his time and the favourite poet of Lorenzo the Magnificent.

The villa has been altered and enlarged since Poliziano's time, but there is a room where he is said to have slept and water still gushes out of the wall into an old stone basin there. In the last few hundred years the house has passed through many hands – for a long time it was a convent and once it was the country place of a Cardinal – and now no other relics are left except the curious atmosphere of the building and the legend of Poliziano himself.

He was an extraordinary man. It was natural enough that I should have grown interested in him since I have been living in the Villa Diana for the past two years; but I became really engrossed one day last summer when I saw the portrait of him painted by Ghirlandaio in the Sassetti Chapel of the Church of Santa Trinita in Florence. It stands fairly high up on the wall behind the altar, but on a fine morning when the sunshine lights upon it from the upper windows, Poliziano comes to life more vividly than he could do in any other way.

He stands in the forefront of the fresco, his long red cloak buttoned up to his neck, emerging from a flight of stairs with his pupil, Giuliano de Medici, Lorenzo's third son, at his side. The portrait of this boy, turning to gaze out of the picture with his confident and trusting eyes, is so enchanting that one immediately fixes one's attention there as though responding instinctively to that innocent and casual glance. Then, with a shock, one looks up into the face of his tutor above. One sees a man with a huge, hooked nose, a fleshy jowl and down-drawn sensual lips.

His long dark hair straggles untidily over his shoulders, and he is gazing upwards at his patron Lorenzo the Magnificent with an expression of passionate devotion. It is a startling face, half predatory and half apologetic, extremely intellectual, and in that one squinting black eye there is a look of timidity and cruelty of the most subtle kind.

Nearly everyone else in the painting is gazing at its main subject, Pope Honorius III, giving his benediction to St Francis. For Poliziano, however, nobody else exists in the room but Lorenzo; and Lorenzo himself, with one hand outstretched, seems to be acknowledging this devotion with a quietly amused air. The story of Poliziano's life is contained in that single, brilliant phrase of painting.

He was born on 14 July 1454 at Montepulciano, the hill town in southern Tuscany where some of the finest Italian wines are grown. At first he was known as Agnolo (or Angelo) Ambrogini, but he changed this later to Poliziano, which is a Latinised version of Montepulciano. The family lived very comfortably in a house on the city walls – one can see it still, a solid fourteenth-century building, in what is now known as the Via Poliziano. Several Italian families are living there at the present time, and except for an inscription over the front door, all evidence of the Ambrogini has long since disappeared.

Poliziano's father, Benedetto Ambrogini, must have been a man of some standing, for he was Gonfaloniere of the city and a judge; but he became involved in a local vendetta and one day he was ambushed and murdered. Little Angelo, then aged nine, saw it happen. He saw the murderers drag his father down to the ground, thrust their pikes into his body, and finally cut his throat.

It has been the custom now for some time – just on five hundred years to be more exact – to regard Poliziano as rather a deplorable character, above all a coward. Yet the chances are that it all began on this summer evening when he saw his father lying bleeding on the ground. From that moment he was oppressed with a nightmarish horror of violence and a deep sense of his personal defencelessness. He never again felt secure, unless there was someone in the background to protect him. He was the opposite of the Benvenuto Cellini sort of character who accepted the violence of the times and made a sport of it. Poliziano was simply frightened. Moreover the other dominating influence on his life – his almost pathological hatred of poverty and his hunger for fame – began to operate immediately after his father's death. He was the eldest of five children all under ten, and Benedetto's widow was quite unable to cope with them all. She packed Angelo off to stay with a poor relation in Florence.

Florence then was a wonderful place in which to live – perhaps more wonderful than any place before or since. It was a city of just 100,000 people, spread across both banks of the Arno, the Arno itself spanned by four bridges, and the whole enclosed in a long towered and crenellated wall that sprawled, lizard-like, across the surrounding hills. The Brunelleschi dome, one of the marvels of the world, had been completed 28 years before, and many of the most elegant buildings of Florence were already standing then. Already the palaces and churches were filled with the work of Giotto, Masaccio, Orcagna, Ghiberti, Donatello, Fra Angelico and Lippo Lippi.

Along the narrow streets every other house was a workshop; the place rang with the labour of goldsmiths, weavers, sculptors and other craftsmen, all carrying out works of original design – and in such quantity that even after the city came to be looted and looted again, and half the great houses and institutions of Europe were furnished with its treasures, there would still be enough left over to preserve Florence as one of the chief repositories of the most beautiful things in the world.

It was, of course, the perfect moment to arrive – the height of that brief sunburst of the human intellect in the Renaissance when every scholar and artist was hastening to Florence; the Medicis were firmly established in power and the Florentine florin was a harder currency than the dollar is to-day.

A great deal of money was spent on clothes and entertainments: noblemen appeared at their dinners and jousts in marvellous three-decker hats and brilliant cloaks. Their retainers were dressed in parti-coloured padded stockings, pointed shoes and feathered caps. The women used every sort of cosmetic, even for their teeth and eyelids. For both sexes there was a vogue for long hair, even false hair, made of white or yellow silk, and the ideal colour was blonde. The love of country life – the 'villa tradition' – had been revived in the surrounding hills; and at this time, when muddy earthen alleys were the usual thing in the other cities of Europe, the streets of Florence were paved and the wealthier people moved about on horseback or in litters and carts.

There was a comfort inside the houses which was unknown in the barbarous cities of France and England – soft beds, carpets, linen, attractive furniture and an enterprising interest in cooking. Centuries after this, it was an odd thing for anyone to take a bath; here in Florence in 1464, the year that Poliziano arrived, people bathed all the time. Diseases like syphilis had not yet arrived (though it did turn up in Naples a few years later, and people were ingenuous enough to think it was a kind of fever in the air). There was, of course, a formidable number of prostitutes, but the Florentines were not especially libertine – they were too busy and too interested in life. In any case the family tradition was very strong and few men would have broken up their households for their mistresses.

All this then was a very fine atmosphere for an ambitious boy about to make a start in life. But Poliziano loathed it. He was lonely and unhappy. When he first arrived, aged ten, he was taken to his uncle's house in the Via Saturnia in one of the poorest districts of the city, on the left bank of the river. The lower part of the building had been let off to some stone masons, and he and his uncle lodged in miserable rooms under the roof. Poliziano spent the next six or seven years in this place and he never could reconcile himself to the poverty and the squalor. All his earliest verses are about it. From them one builds up a picture of a thin and rather ungainly little boy in a threadbare cloak and cracked shoes trudging across the Ponte Vecchio each morning on his way to school at the Compagnia di Dottrina.

But he was a fantastic scholar, far superior to every other boy in the school. At the age of 12 he was writing and eventually publishing letters in Latin. A year or two later he was producing Latin epigrams and at 16 he embarked on a translation of Homer's *Iliad* into Latin hexameters – an enterprise which had already baffled some of the leading scholars of the day.

He adored his studies, and he was driven on, as he says himself, by a morbid fear that he would have to give them up and go into trade to earn a living. Like most poor and brilliant boys he had a nervous and claustrophobic sense of his own superiority; and a desperate feeling that his talents would never be recognised. All around him he could see that a wonderful life was going on, people were succeeding and enjoying themselves – but how could you break into these enchanted circles if you could not even afford a new pair of shoes? What one needed was a patron. Lorenzo now, in 1469, was aged 21, and he had just opened his reign of the city by winning a notable joust in the Piazza Santa Croce. The chances of a poor student catching his busy eye were not very good; it was much more likely that

Angelo would finish up as a stone-cutter's apprentice in the Via Saturnia.

However, it was Homer who saved him. When Poliziano had finished the second book of the *Iliad* he made a parcel of the manuscript, drew a deep breath no doubt, and sent it off to Lorenzo with the following letter written in Latin:

> *Magnificent Lorenzo, to whom Heaven has given charge of the city and the State, first citizen of Florence, doubly crowned with bays lately for war in San Croce amid the acclamations of the people and for poetry on account of the sweetness of your verses, give ear to me, who drinking at Greek sources, am striving to get Homer into Latin metre. This second book which I have translated (you know we have the first by Messer Carlo d'Arezzo) comes to you and timidly crosses your threshold. If you welcome it I propose to offer you all the 'Iliad.' It rests with you, who can, to help the Poet. I desire no other muse or other gods, but only you; by your help I can do that of which the ancients would not have been ashamed. May it please you, therefore, at your leisure to give audience to Homer...*
>
> *Your servant,*
> *Angelo Poliziano*

Far from being put off by this effusion, Lorenzo read the manuscript, was delighted with it and sent for the author at once. Nobody knows the details of that first interview, but apparently it was a case of something bordering on love at first sight. In the next 23 years there was only one major break in their friendship, and Poliziano was with his patron when he died.

Later on, when the reaction against Lorenzo set in, many sinister stories of Poliziano were spread around. At those Lucullan dinner parties on Fiesole – the page boy strumming on the lute, the wine passing rapidly and the lights of Florence shining down below – he was the one who produced the ripest epigrams and the most abandoned songs. He was the courtier who smiled and smiled – and laughed at all Lorenzo's jokes; the sycophant who could never write so much as a carnival ballad without dedicating it to his master saying how brilliant, how generous and how noble he was. Constantly, so the legend runs, Poliziano was begging for something or other in the choicest Latin and with a brand of lick-spittle humility that went beyond flattery into a new and horrible literature of its own.

All of this, if true, seems to overlook the fact that Lorenzo was an overwhelming character, a kind of universal man, half gay and half intensely serious. He was a poet, a Latinist and a fabulous collector of manuscripts and works of art. He was a farmer, a huntsman and a lover of music. He had a genius for selecting men and getting the best out of them; and, although he was only 21, he already had the rare gift of seeing politics as a temporary and local thing set against a background of permanent philosophy. He was interested in everything, and he could switch from one mood to another, just as some men can wake or fall asleep at a moment's notice.

He had too, that vivacity and patient charm of a man who feels at ease with himself and is quite certain of his place in the world. Apparently it did not matter that he had a dark and ugly face with a slightly twisted mouth and a flattened nose: what one noticed was his remarkable eyes. They had an expression that was something between melancholy and laughter; perhaps this came from the fact that there were intervals in his headlong career when he was in great pain.

To come into the presence of this man in his palace – especially if you were a tattered student aged 16 – must have been an unusual experience, even rather frightening and exciting. At all events from the moment of this first meeting Poliziano became the devoted follower. After this he really did have no other gods but Lorenzo, and the rhetorical praises that he started to heap on Lorenzo were no more than the customary thing. At that time when printing was just beginning, a scholar had to have a patron in order to live, and to keep a patron you had to praise him. It was more of a manner of writing than anything else, and in any event, the feeling was genuine in Poliziano's case.

Lorenzo was five years older than he was and all that sense of security and protection which the boy had been hungering for since his father's death now came flowing back into his life again. Since not even Lorenzo's worst enemies have managed to suggest it, there seems to be no question of a homo-sexual relationship between them; they simply delighted in one another's company.

No doubt Poliziano's teacher, Marsilio Ficino the Platonist, did something to pave the way. 'Proceed with the good work, my Lorenzo,' Ficino wrote. 'Homer, the high priest of the muses, under your auspices has come to Italy. By your noble bounty, you maintain that Homeric youth, Angelo Poliziano, whom you found wandering a beggar over the face of the earth.'

Lorenzo did more than maintain young Homer; he transformed his life. Poliziano was fitted out with new clothes, the best professors were chosen to teach him at the Studio Florentine, and he became a table-companion at the Palazzo Medici. At first he was merely the boy prodigy who was trotted out before the distinguished guests. Later he became a kind of private secretary, helping both Lorenzo and his wife with their correspondence; and in 1473 he was installed in rooms in the palace itself. Soon after this he was made the tutor of Lorenzo's children; later on, with a certain amount of unashamed cadging, he contrived to get possession of the Priory of S. Paolo, a pleasant church that still stands just off the Piazza Santa Maria Novella. This was a snug little benefice, worth a hundred gold florins a year. Poliziano was not over-taxed in his duties there since, for a small fee, he hired someone else to perform them for him.

By now he was getting up in the world; his mother had married again in Montepulciano, the men who had killed his father had been duly murdered in their turn, and, as tutor to the Medici household, he was in an extremely influential position. When Lorenzo went abroad on his hunting expeditions, it was Poliziano's job to write back to his patron's wife, Clarice, telling her what they were up to. There is a certain unaffected naturalness about these letters which was rare for those days and rarer still for Poliziano.

Magnifica Domina mea, he wrote once from Pisa. *I did not write yesterday to Your Magnificence, because Lorenzo sent me to Lucca. I have just come back and take up my pen to keep faith with you. Lorenzo is well and in good spirits. Yesterday there was little wind and he went hawking; but they had not much luck because the young falcon belonging to Pilato, called the Mantuan, was lost. This morning they went out again, but the wind was not favourable; nevertheless, we saw some fine flights, and Maestro Giorgio flew his peregrine falcon which came back to the lure most obediently. Lorenzo is quite in love with it. Of a truth he is not wrong, for Maestro Giorgio says he never saw a handsomer or a better, and declares he will make of him the finest falcon in the world. While we were in the fields, Pilato came back from the river with his lost falcon, so Lorenzo was doubly pleased. If I knew what to write I should be glad; but I can only give you news of this hawking as we do nothing else in the morning and the afternoon. This evening I hear that on Monday Lorenzo intends to hunt roe deer and then return at once to Florence. Please God we may find you well and with a boy in your arms.*

(They almost did: Lorenzo's second son, who afterwards, became Pope Leo X, was born ten days later.)

I commend myself to Your Magnificence. In Pisa, December 1,
1475
Angelo da Montepulciano

But it is the happy letter written by Poliziano to Clarice from San Miniato that gives the full flavour of these early days.

Magnifica Domina mea, he says. *Yesterday, after leaving*
Florence, we came as far as San Miniato singing all the way, and
occasionally talking of holy things so as not to forget Lent. At
Lastra we drank zappolino, which tasted much better than I had
been told. Lorenzo is brilliant and makes the whole company gay:
yesterday I counted twenty-six horses which are with him. When
we reached San Miniato last evening we began to read a little of
S. Augustine, then the reading resolved itself into music, and
looking at and instructing a certain well-known dancer who is
here. Lorenzo is just going to Mass. I will finish another time.
At San Miniato. April 8 (1476). Servitor.
Your Angelo

Up to this time there was no sign of the famous row that developed later between Poliziano and Clarice; indeed there were no clouds on Poliziano's horizon at all. He was an established wit at the Medici dinner table and the companion of Lorenzo on some of his more worldly adventures in the midnight streets of Florence. He was developing from a student into a poet. And he was involved in all the elaborate carnivals and parades with which Lorenzo is supposed to have debauched the Florentines in the early part of his reign. Many of the songs which were sung by the actors at these performances were composed by Poliziano and some of the best of them have a charming quality, reminding one strongly of Herrick, with perhaps a little Spenser added.

One of the most famous of them begins:

Ben venga maggio
E l'gonfalon selvaggio.

Then there is the ballad about the garden:

I' mi trovai un di tutto soletto
In un bel prato per pigliar diletto…

And such light-hearted lines as *Dagli occhi del labella Leoncina*, which he wrote in praise of the Florentine girls. There are dozens of ballads like these and they still sound as spontaneous and artless as a milk boy's whistle in the morning.

Certainly the theme was slight enough. In all these verses Poliziano is constantly finding himself in some delectable garden or stretch of the hillside surrounded by spring flowers and dizzy with love. A beautiful and simple country girl appears (usually referred to as a nymph). He is on fire at once and it will be madness, says the poet, if the girl resists him. A slight chase through the woods is permissible, but if she keeps it up too long she will discover that nobody wants to chase her anyway.

It was Lorenzo himself who set the fashion for this sort of thing with his:

Quant' e bella giovinezza
Che si fugge tuttavia
Chi vuol' esser lieto sia
Di doman non ci è certezza.

Which is probably best translated by Herrick's –

Gather ye rose-buds while ye may,
Old Time is still a-flying:
And this same flower that smiles to-day,
Tomorrow will be dying.

Not all their songs were as innocent as this, and the carnivals themselves were apt to be hilarious affairs. In the decorated cars that passed down the streets there were representations of pagan gods and goddesses, devils, imps, nuns escaping from convents, satyrs pursuing nymphs, clowns, idiots, wild beasts and gypsies. Often there were allegorical figures depicting the four ages of man, the winds and the elements, in addition to fertility rites and phallic symbols. For all these Poliziano wrote songs – ironic, witty or downright bawdy – and a quantity of much more serious verse as well. Presently, he embarked on a much longer piece which was to establish his name as the greatest poet of the day. This was his *Stanze*.

The *Stanze* were supposed to be written for the tournament of Giuliano de' Medici, Lorenzo's young brother, but they never arrive at a description of the tournament at all. Instead they are a panegyric in the classical manner – perhaps Pope is the nearest English equivalent – of Giuliano's love for his mistress, Simonetta Vespucci.

The appearance of this girl in Florence somewhere about 1469 apparently caused a sensation, but no amount of research really gets you very far with her story. She remains one of those legends in the Helen of Troy tradition, and it is difficult to find the point where literary figures like Poliziano got hold of the facts and pushed them a good deal further than history will strictly allow.

However, it seems certain that Simonetta was born of a well-connected family in Genoa, about 1453, and the register of the church of Santa Maria Novella in Florence shows that she was married to Marco Vespucci there in 1469, when they were both aged 16. Her dowry consisted of a share in some mines at Piombino. At the time of the tournament (when she was 22), she is described as Giuliano's mistress, which may have been true enough for Giuliano had a number of love affairs. But then again she may have been Lorenzo's mistress or even the mistress of Botticelli, for Simonetta was the most beautiful and adored girl in Florence. Half the artists of the time are said to have painted her, every poet sang songs to her, and all the more eligible young men are supposed to have been in love with her. The whole city was charmed and delighted whenever she appeared. There is a possible parallel in the delirious atmosphere that surrounds a film star at the present time.

This was the age of pretty girls in Florence, and it was the fashion to talk and dream about them; Simonetta was the phenomenal flower that suddenly and mysteriously out-matches all the rest. She had blue eyes, golden hair and the most delicate skin. She was unaffected and simple and kind. And in spite of all the talk about her lovers she was chaste as well as beautiful. Lorenzo even said she had the supreme virtue: 'All men praised her and no woman abused her.'

Clearly, at this distance, it is a hopeless business to try and separate the actual girl from the myth; and perhaps even then the myth was almost as real as Simonetta herself. Most of the young poets and artists round Lorenzo were full of their rediscovery of ancient Greece, and it was not long before La Bella Simonetta was being glamorised into a second Venus – here she was again, the Goddess of Love, the pagan Virgin.

Poliziano, aged 21 and full of Hellenic visions, plunged into this mood with gusto, and the Simonetta myth is probably more his creation than that of anybody else.

The whole contraption of nymphs, fauns, and woodland groves fascinated him, and at this time, while he was still hewing away at Homer, he was searching about for fresh inspiration. Giuliano's tournament alone would not have been enough, but it was followed by the aesthetically perfect event – Simonetta died.

This happened 12 months after the tournament. Lorenzo had sent his personal physician to attend her. But Simonetta, like so many beautiful girls, was consumptive, and on the night of 26 April 1476, she died at the age of 23.

All Florence went into mourning. In tears great crowds followed the funeral to the Church of the Ognissanti, on the banks of the Arno. The bier was left open and in the springtime sunshine the people looked down for the last time on the blonde curls blowing around the miraculously lovely face.

Poliziano abandoned his Homer and embarked at once on his poem. It consists of 173 stanzas, divided into two cantos, and it has no set theme or any attempt at reality; it is simply a series of scenes from the Greek myths. Nymphs and satyrs abound, gods and goddesses cavort through classical gardens, with cupids in their wake; and all this is done with a kind of highly-polished brilliance that almost comes nearer painting than writing. If you take the verses one by one you get nothing but a stream of starry words, half meaningless in themselves; repeat the whole stanza and it comes perfectly into focus. This kind of exquisite dove-tailing is not the easiest thing to reproduce in English. It is a pity that Rossetti, who translated so many of the earlier Italian poets, never attempted it, for none of the translations made by others have been successful.

Technically the great interest of the poem is that it perfected the eight-line stanza in the Italian language (it rhymes Abababcc) and in this, as in its general treatment, it set the fashion for verse for the next hundred years or more. It is regarded now as one of the finest lyrical poems in Italian literature, and from the first it had a phenomenal success. Some of the greatest artists of the Renaissance – Piero di Cosimo, Leonardo da Vinci, Giulio Romano and even Raphael – are reputed to have painted canvases from scenes in the *Stanze*. The most famous passages, of course, are those that depict Simonetta in the springtime forest, and the description of Venus riding on a shell towards the shore. From these Botticelli painted his *Primavera* and his *Birth of Venus*, which are now practically the best-known possessions of the Uffizi Gallery in Florence. An elaborate controversy still rages among scholars as to just how far Botticelli painted Poliziano's exact words, and how far he simply used them as a spring-board for his own imagination.

However, to the layman's eye, both pictures seem remarkably faithful to the poem. In the *Primavera* Simonetta is supposed to be the third figure from the right, blonde and enigmatically beautiful. She wears a flowered white robe, precisely as Poliziano described her – *Candida è ella è Candida la vesta*. In the *Birth of Venus*, Simonetta is not supposed to be Venus herself, but the nymph on the right, holding out the robe to her. Neither of these two figures, however, bears much resemblance to the authentic portrait of Simonetta which Ghirlandaio painted in the Ognissanti Church, where she is buried. Ghirlandaio painted a pale and fragile girl with a plucked hair-line – a fashion which was popular at the time, but is slightly repellent to modern taste.

Like the poem itself, with its fantastic mannered brilliance, the Botticelli paintings have undergone an erratic series of ups and downs in popularity during the last five hundred years. There have been times when people discovered that they were the perfect expression of that rose-coloured glow that spread over Renaissance Florence, the romantic paganism and the aching, adolescent sense of beauty. At other moments, and for no given reason, popular taste has swung the other way and Botticelli was regarded as too fanciful and too lyrical, perhaps even decadent. Now, in the Atomic Age, his popularity is immense. If you go into the Uffizi Gallery at any hour of the day you will be sure to find an eager group of tourists gazing up at that shy and delicate figure of Venus as though it were something seen in a dream – not real, but yet conveying so much more than this present mechanical life around us.

Poliziano, no doubt, would have written a good deal more on these themes, had he been given a chance, and, in fact, he was still at work on the poem when, on the morning of 26 April 1478, the anniversary of Simonetta's death, his hero Giuliano was murdered in the cathedral.

After that, there was not much opportunity for Poliziano or anyone else in Florence to feel very romantic for some time to come.

The Pazzi Conspiracy was, of course, a great deal more than a simple vendetta; it was a deliberate plot on the part of Pope Sixtus IV, the Pazzi family and a number of others to murder Lorenzo and Giuliano and seize control of Florence. Its importance in Poliziano's life is that it brought him back into the arena of physical violence and that was where he never showed himself at his best. There is the hint of the frightened man in the way he writes of the events of that drastic morning.

According to Poliziano, the Pazzi brothers and the other plotters decided to make their attack in the cathedral at Florence, just when Lorenzo and Giuliano were kneeling before the altar at High Mass: and the raising of the Host was to be the signal for them to strike. Since all the plotters were their guests, Lorenzo and Giuliano suspected nothing. But, says Poliziano, Giuliano was ill and failed to turn up at the last moment when everyone else was filing into the cathedral. Two of the conspirators then hastened off to Giuliano's house and persuaded him to come. As they passed into the cathedral they affectionately put their arms round Giuliano's shoulders to make sure that he was not wearing a coat of mail.

Mass began. Lorenzo and Giuliano knelt and the Host was raised. Immediately Giuliano was felled with a terrible dagger thrust in his chest. Nevertheless, he got up, says Poliziano, 'ran a few steps, but they followed him. Then, losing consciousness, the poor boy fell to the ground, where Francesco Pazzi stabbed at him again and again with his dagger and thus horribly murdered him.'

Meanwhile, Lorenzo too, had been hit in the neck, but not so badly. He jumped up, wound his cloak round his left arm as a shield and pulled out his sword. Then with one or two others, he managed to fight his way back into the sacristy. Poliziano ran into the sacristy with them, and the heavy doors were closed and bolted.

By this time the cathedral was in an uproar, priests, women and children flying in all directions and crying out that the roof was falling in. Those who were inside the sacristy with Lorenzo could see nothing, and consequently had no idea of what was happening.

'While we stood on guard at the door,' Poliziano goes on, 'some of us grew anxious about Lorenzo's wound, and, fearing that the dagger which made it was poisoned, Antonio Ridolfo, the son of Jacopo, a brave young man, began to suck it. Lorenzo, however, paid no attention to it and kept asking: "Is Giuliano safe?" and he angrily threatened and complained against the men who had betrayed him. Suddenly many young supporters gathered outside the sacristy door crying out that they were friends and relatives, that Lorenzo, at all costs, should come out before his opponents could gather strength. We inside were suspicious, not knowing whether they were friends or enemies, but we kept asking them continually if Giuliano was safe. To this they made no reply.'

In the end, however, one of Lorenzo's attendants climbed the ladders to the organ loft, where he looked down into the cathedral. He saw Giuliano's body lying on the floor and he saw that the men outside the sacristy were, in fact, friends. Then he called down to the others to open the doors. Lorenzo's men posted themselves around him so that he could not see his brother's body and conducted him home to the Medici Palace.

'I myself,' says Poliziano, 'returning to my house by a direct route, saw the body full of wounds, all bleeding and horribly dead. Trembling and uncertain and almost out of my mind with the enormity of the tragedy, I was helped by some friends, who accompanied me to my house.'

According to other accounts, Poliziano was demoralised by the scene and fainted clean away on the cathedral floor. At all events, he took no further part in the happenings for the moment, while fighting continued through the streets of Florence. A mob gathered outside the Medici Palace and to reassure them Lorenzo appeared on a balcony with his neck bandaged.

When things had quietened down, Poliziano emerged again and went to the Piazza Signoria. There he saw the aftermath of a bloody struggle. Those conspirators who had been chosen to seize the Palazzo Vecchio – the seat of the government – while the Medicis were being attacked in the cathedral had been beaten off. Many of them had been captured, hacked to death with pikes and swords, and then hung by their necks from the balconies of the palace. Soldiers were now busy cutting down the bodies and dragging them through the streets. For the moment the victory of the Medici was complete.

There followed through the rest of that catastrophic spring and summer of 1478 the excommunication of Florence by the Pope on 7 June, the plague and the war. On 13 July a Neapolitan herald arrived at the city gates and on behalf of the Pope and the King of Naples declared war on Florence, unless it chose to expel Lorenzo, 'to which,' says one of the diarists of the time, 'the citizens would not agree, and so war began'.

The principal effect of all this on Poliziano was that he was sent off with Lorenzo's wife and her children to take refuge outside the city on a country estate near Pistoia. No doubt he was glad to go at first. Carnivals, tournaments and the singing of ballads had stopped abruptly and Florence became a dismal city, no place for a poet or a scholar. The long, rose-coloured springtime of Lorenzo's early reign was over and it seemed to Poliziano, cooped up in the country with nobody to talk to, that the reason for his own existence had vanished as well. He was just 24 and he was beginning to discover again what life was like without Lorenzo.

II

One of the surprising things about Angelo Poliziano is that he remained to the end of his life a hopeless politician.

Although he lived for more than twenty years with Lorenzo the Magnificent, the shrewdest and most tactful diplomatist of the Renaissance, he apparently learned nothing whatever of the art of dealing with other men. Usually, he had just two reactions: one was adoration and the other was loathing, and he shifted from one to the other with abandon.

When he had arrived as a young man at the Medici Court in Florence, the first thing he wanted to do was to write a triumphal ode in the style of Homer's *Iliad*, in honour of Lorenzo's capture of Volterra. Since this was a cruel and unnecessary campaign, one of the few blunders of Lorenzo's career, it seems hardly likely that the Medicis would have wanted it commemorated in heroic verse; and, in fact, if the poem was ever written, it never appeared. Later on at the height of Poliziano's fame, when he was practically the dictator of Italian letters, he still went on making enemies and taking wrong decisions. At his death, one of his contemporaries remarked tartly: 'The wonder is not that at sixteen Poliziano knew a thousand times more than one usually knows at that age, but that at forty he knew nothing more.'

The worst of these many crises in Poliziano's life, the one that very nearly wrecked his career, occurred in the summer of 1478 when, of all people, he chose to make an enemy of Clarice Orsini, Lorenzo's wife. Apart from everything else, it was a very bad moment to start such a quarrel, since Lorenzo was then deeply involved in his losing struggle against the Pope and the King of Naples.

As wars go, this was not a very bitter affair, since it was fought on both sides by mercenary soldiers, who were none too keen to get to grips with one another. Probably at this stage, Florence was in no real danger, but soon plague broke out in the city and Lorenzo judged it wiser to keep his family out in the country, near Pistoia.

The party which had gone down to Pistoia consisted of Clarice and her six children – the two boys Piero and Giovanni, and the four girls, Lucrezia, Luisa, Maddalena and Contessina. Poliziano's job was to tutor the two boys; and this was where the trouble began. Clarice wanted them taught the scriptures; Poliziano was all for Latin and Greek. She kept interfering. No sooner had Poliziano set the boys an exercise, than Clarice called them off and put them on something else. Already, in August, Poliziano began protesting to Lorenzo that his position was becoming intolerable: he was prepared to put up with it for Lorenzo's sake, he wrote, but it was impossible to avoid constant collisions with Clarice. Surely, now the war was on, Lorenzo could find him some more important job in Florence?

Lorenzo seems to have made no reply to this, and the quarrels dragged on through September. Clarice was pregnant again and often she had to take to her bed. But directly she got up she renewed the attack. Through September there is a rising note of irritation in Poliziano's letters to Lorenzo. Probably he was forced to submit these letters to Clarice's censorship before he sent them off, and he soon began to develop a rather nasty trick of slipping into either Latin or Greek (which Clarice could not read) if he wanted to say anything unpleasant.

'The children play more than usual and are in splendid health,' he says in one of the earlier letters. 'God help them and you. Piero never leaves me or I him. I wish I had to serve you in some more important way, but this has fallen to my lot, and I do it willingly.'

Then he goes on in Latin: 'But I beg you to ensure, either by letter or messenger, that my authority shall not be restricted, so that I can more easily guide the boy and fulfil my duty.'

But the real origins of the row went a good deal deeper than a mere squabble in the children's schoolroom. Clarice and Poliziano were hopelessly ill-adjusted. Poliziano was a nervous, ambitious, highly intellectual character who had jumped into Lorenzo's favour from the obscure back streets of Florence, and he had a sarcastic tongue. Clarice was the daughter of a patrician Roman family with a strictly religious background, and she had an instinctive dislike for these bright young Florentine intellectuals.

There is something desperately pathetic about Clarice. Yet for some reason – perhaps because the list of her worries is too long and too complete – it is difficult to feel as sorry for her as one ought to be. She is the apotheosis of neglected wives. Married to a brilliant man, whose friends she never quite liked or understood, saddled with too many children too quickly, suffering from consumption and probably well aware of Lorenzo's love affairs, there never seems to have been a moment when she could relax with a quiet mind. Lorenzo was always sending her away somewhere or going away himself, and because she loved him, she pursued him with sad little notes: 'There is nothing of importance to tell you except that we are waiting to see you again. When will you come?'

She never felt completely at home among the Florentines; her home was in Rome and her faith was strongly in the church. Now her husband was not only at war with Rome, but he had been excommunicated by the Pope as well. With her Orsini blood, Clarice was much too proud to submit tamely and there were moments when she was driven beyond endurance (as Poliziano was about to find out); but somehow her protests sounded feeble. She gives the impression of forever trying to catch up, of always being a little uncertain of herself. Lorenzo never humiliated her and his letters are full of affection, but they lack warmth. He treated this marriage for what it was – a political arrangement between two great families – and he was fond of Clarice, but without passion.

She had the misfortune, too, to be over-shadowed by her remarkable mother-in-law, Madonna Lucrezia. It was Lucrezia's cold, shrewd, motherly eye which had first fallen on Clarice when the Medici were hunting about for a wife for Lorenzo 11 years before. At that time, on 27 March 1467, Lucrezia had written to her husband, Piero, from Rome:

On the way to St Peter's on Thursday morning, I met Madonna Maddalena Orsini, sister to the Cardinal, with her daughter, who is about fifteen or sixteen years old. She was dressed in the Roman fashion with a lenzuolo (a loose shawl). *In this dress she seemed to me to be handsome, fair and tall, but being so covered up I could not see her to my satisfaction.*

Yesterday I paid a visit to the said Monsignor Orsini in his sister's house, which joins his. When I saluted him in your name, his sister came in with the maiden, who had on a tight frock in the fashion of Rome without the lenzuolo. We talked for some time and I looked closely at the girl. As I said, she is of good height and has a nice complexion, her manners are gentle, though not so winning as those of our girls, but she is very modest and would soon learn our customs. She has not fair hair, because there are no fair women; her hair is reddish and abundant, her face rather round, but it does not displease me. Her throat is fairly elegant, but it seems to me a little meagre, or, so to speak, slight. Her bosom I could not see, as here the women are entirely covered up, but it appeared to me of good proportions. She does not carry her head proudly like our girls, but pokes it forward a little: I think she was shy. Indeed I see no fault in her except shyness.

Her hands are long and delicate. In short, I think, the girl is much above the common, though she cannot compare with Maria, Lucrezia and Bianca (Lucrezia's own daughters). *Lorenzo has seen her and you can find out whether she pleases him. Whatever he and you decide will be well done and I shall be content. Let us leave the issue to God.*

There follows a list of the estates of the Orsini family and a pretty good hint that a substantial dowry could be expected.

Lorenzo and Clarice were married in Florence in June, 1469, at a series of ceremonies that went on for five days and nights. Clarice wore a robe of white and gold brocade, and there were over a thousand guests, who danced in a special pavilion in the streets and consumed a hundred barrels of wine a day.

In the nine years since then the long process of disillusionment had set in. Clarice still loved Lorenzo and she missed him terribly at times – especially now that he was in danger in Florence and she was isolated in the country at Pistoia. Poliziano's presence only made matters worse. He was Lorenzio's choice of a tutor, not hers; and no doubt she was irritated by his toadying to Lorenzo and his literary airs.

Poliziano, on his side, was longing to get back to Lorenzo and his gay friends in Florence. He was still young enough and impetuous enough to think that he could laugh at Clarice and occasionally defy her. In fact, he was making the fatal mistake of not only underrating his patron's wife, but all the other people who were also jealous of his intimacy with Lorenzo.

The quarrel was simmering steadily at the end of the summer, when suddenly the family were warned that the enemy was approaching Pistoia itself. They decamped at once to the castle-fortress of Cafaggiuolo, about a day's journey north of Florence. It was already November when they made the trip, and all of them loathed it.

Clarice, Poliziano and the children were now joined by an old friend of the family, Gentile Becchi, and in a long caravan of doctors, attendants, and men-at-arms, they trundled over the mountains in coaches and on horseback.

Even at the present time, when the main road to Bologna runs past the front door and Florence is only an hour away by car, Cafaggiuolo is not a very cheerful place in winter. It lies low down at the head of the Mugello valley among damp river flats. The Medici Castle, which was built by Michelozzo, has been converted into a state agricultural centre in recent years and piles of grain have been dumped into the rooms where Clarice and Poliziano lived and the children used to play. After five hundred years the building is still sound, but damp is creeping in and cracks have begun to develop in the tower.

The rooms are large, square and very lofty, the floors are of stone, and in the fifteenth century no great attention was paid to draughts or heating. There is still no township there – just this one beautiful castle with its outhouses. The Trebbio castle-fortress, another of the Medici possessions, stands a few kilometres away on the crest of a sharp hill overlooking Cafaggiuolo and the valley. To reach either place one has to climb a ridge of mountains from Florence, and in Lorenzo's time the roads were so bad that travellers were often held up for several days. During December and

January the icy wind rages for days on end, and it is often accompanied by persistent rain and thunderstorms.

Lorenzo's mother, Madonna Lucrezia, remained in Florence – one can imagine the old lady refusing to budge – and very soon the family were writing to her that they were 'up to their necks in water' and forced to stay indoors all day.

Poliziano enjoyed country life well enough, but he preferred it in the spring, preferably with a nymph sporting about through the wild flowers and the prospect of an amusing dinner party with Lorenzo at the end of the day. Exasperated by the weather and bored to death by the domestic atmosphere of Clarice and her children, he sent off this distraught letter to Madonna Lucrezia in the middle of December:

Magnifica Domina Mea –

The news from this place is that it rains violently and incessantly, so that it is impossible to leave the house, and instead of hunting we have taken to playing ball, so that the children can exercise. We generally play for the soup, the sweet or the meat; and he who loses goes without. Often, when one of my scholars loses, he cries. I have no other news to give you. I sit by the fire in dressing gown and slippers and were you to see me you would think that I was melancholy personified; for that is what I seem to myself. I neither do nor see nor hear anything that gives me pleasure, so much have I taken our calamities to heart. Sleeping and waking they haunt me. Two days ago we began to spread our wings, for we heard the plague had ceased; now we are down again because it is still said to be going about. In Florence we have some sort of comfort, if only that of seeing Lorenzo come home safe and well. Here we are in perpetual anxiety about everything, and I assure you I am dying of, melancholy, such is my solitude. I say solitude because Monsignore (Becchi) *shuts himself up in his own room with only his thoughts for company, and I always find him so cast down and full of care that my own melancholy is increased in his company.*

Ser Alberto di Malerba (a priest who had joined them) *mumbles prayers with the children all day long, so I remain alone, and when I am tired of study I ring the changes on plague and war, on grief for the past and fear for the future, and have no one with whom to air my fantasies. I do not find my Madonna Lucrezia in her room, with whom I can unbosom myself and I am bored to death... However, I am trying to arm myself with hope and cling to everything in order not to sink to the bottom. I have nothing else to say. I commend myself to Your Magnificence — Cafaggiuolo December 18, 1478. Servitor.*

Angelus

Through January 1479 he killed time by composing a Latin ode, keeping a diary of jottings (it is full of nostalgic bright sayings he remembered from Lorenzo's dinner-table) writing his version of the Pazzi conspiracy and bickering with Clarice; and still the rain poured down. Clarice's child was born at last on a brief visit to Florence in February, and they named it Giuliano, after Lorenzo's murdered younger brother. While Clarice was in Florence, Poliziano snatched his pupils away from Ser Alberto, the mumbling priest, and put them back on to the classical languages. But directly Clarice returned to Cafaggiuolo, she reversed all this, and by April things were moving rapidly towards an open breach. Poliziano protested to Lorenzo:

As for Giovanni (the second boy, who became Pope Leo X), *you will have seen for yourself. His mother has taken it upon herself to change his course of reading to the Psalter, a thing I did not approve of. While she was absent he had made wonderful progress.*

This was true enough; Poliziano had been pushing both boys through a course of Latin and Greek which would have made a modern schoolboy shudder. Piero, the eldest, was only eight at this time and his letters to his father from Cafaggiuolo have a remarkable maturity.

Magnificent Father, he wrote, *Lucrezia and I are competing to see who can write best. She is writing to grandmother Lucrezia, I, my father, to you. The one who gets what he asks for wins. Until now Lucrezia has had everything she wanted. I, who have always written in Latin, in order to give a more literary tone to my letters, have not had that pony you promised me; and so I am laughed at by everyone. See to it, therefore, Your Magnificence, that she is not always the winner.*

This letter was dated 26 May 1479, and it is followed by another, which is undated, except for the year:

Magnificent Father Mine – That pony does not come, and I am afraid that it will remain so long with you, that Andrea will cause it to change from a beast into a man. We are all well and studying. Giovanni is beginning to spell. By this letter you can judge how I am writing... Giuliano laughs and thinks of nothing else; Lucrezia sews, sings and reads; Maddalena knocks her head against the wall, but without hurting herself; Luisa begins to say a few little words; Contessina fills the house with her noise. All the others attend to their duties and we need nothing except your presence. We heard that things are better than last year, and hope that, you being well, there will be nothing but victory in the future. Strong and brave men are not good at subterfuges, but shine in open warfare. Thus we confide in you, as we all know that besides your goodness and valour, you bear in mind the heritage left us by our ancestors and the injury and outrages we have endured.

God save you – Your son Piero.

Then this:

Magnificent Father Mine – I fear that some misfortune has happened to that pony, for had it been well I know you would have sent it me as you promised. I beg, therefore, as a grace, that you will take this fear away from me; for I think of it day and night, and until the pony comes I shall have no peace. In case

*the original one cannot come, please send me another. For, as I
have already written you, I am here on foot, and sometimes it is
necessary for me to go off in the company of my friends. See to
this, therefore, Your Magnificence.*

Finally:

*Magnifico Patrio meo — I cannot tell you, Magnificent Father,
how glad I am to have the pony, and how his arrival stimulates
me to work. If I desire to praise him, 'Ante diem clause Olympo.'
He is so handsome and perfect, that the trumpet of Maronius
would hardly be enough to sing his praises. You can imagine how
I love him — especially when his joyous neighs resound and rejoice
the whole neighbourhood. I owe you and send you many thanks
for such a fine gift, and I shall try to repay you by becoming what
you wish. Of this you may be sure. I promise that I shall try with
all my heart. We are all well, and we long for your arrival.*
  God save you — Your son, Piero.

Meanwhile, Clarice had thrown Poliziano out of the house.
The final row must have been bitter, since Clarice, for once,
did not wait to consult Lorenzo. Little Piero at one stage
appears to have supported his tutor. Much later he declared
that his mother was not to blame and that Poliziano used
to shout at her. At all events Poliziano left the castle in such
a remarkable hurry that he even abandoned his books.

He did not dare to go straight to Florence without
Lorenzo's permission, nor did he care to approach

Lorenzo until he had prepared the way; and so he made for another of the Medici villas at Careggi, just outside Florence, hoping, no doubt, to find Lorenzo's mother, Madonna Lucrezia, there. Lucrezia was a poet herself, and had always been a good friend of his. It was spring again, the first week in May, the month Poliziano used to sing about so blithely in the old days. This crestfallen little note was delivered to Lorenzo in Florence:

Magnifice mi domine – I am here at Careggi, having left Cafaggiuolo by command of Madonna Clarice. The cause and manner of my departure I desire – indeed I beg – to be allowed to explain by word of mouth, it is too long to write. When you have heard me I think you will admit that the fault is not all mine. For decency's sake and not wishing to go to Florence without your orders, I came here and am waiting till Your Magnificence informs me what I am to do, because I am yours, even if the whole world were against me. If I have had only small success in serving you, it was not that I did not serve with all my heart. I commend myself to Your Magnificence and am entirely at your commands.

Careggi May 6 1479. Ever Your Magnificence's servant.
Angelus Pol

This put Lorenzo in an awkward position. He was too fond of Poliziano to throw him over entirely; at the same time he could not humiliate Clarice by taking his side. In the end he compromised by installing Poliziano as librarian at the

Medici quarters on the hill of Fiesole. Poliziano at once began throwing off epigrams in praise of his patron, and it is not difficult to imagine the sort of gossip he spread about Clarice among his friends. Soon the whole court knew about the quarrel, and Matteo Franco, the poet, permitted himself to make a joke which came to Clarice's ears. She was furious.

I should be glad not to be turned into ridicule by Franco…, she wrote to Lorenzo on 28 May, *and also that Messer Angelo should not be able to boast that he lives in your house whether I like it or not; and that you have put him into your own room at Fiesole. You know I told you that if you wished him to remain I was perfectly content, and although I have endured a thousand insults, if it has been by your permission, I am content; but this I can hardly believe.*

In her exasperation Clarice began to put herself in the wrong by refusing to give up Poliziano's books which he had left behind at Cafaggiuolo – they included the Homer, Plato and Demosthenes which he had prepared for Piero, his interpretations and addresses to Lorenzo and a quantity of other private manuscripts. Clarice claimed that since the books were prepared for Piero, they were Medici property, and Poliziano was now complaining loudly; he even got Lorenzo's secretary to demand the books back. Clarice ignored this. Things had reached the point where only Lorenzo himself could pacify her, and at last, at the end of May, he visited Cafaggiuolo. Poliziano, he insisted to Clarice, was to stay at Fiesole and he was to have his books; but she would not be forced to take him back as tutor, and he would see to it that Poliziano did not annoy her. With this Clarice had to be content, and Lorenzo hurried back to Florence and the war again.

The first round then was clearly Poliziano's. But he had won it at the cost of making a permanent enemy of Clarice, and there were a good many others in the Medici household who thought he was getting too big for his boots. In Fiesole, he began to notice a certain coolness in the air. Lorenzo was charming to him whenever they met, but he kept him in suspense about the future. Whenever Poliziano started agitating to be re-appointed as tutor, Lorenzo was extremely vague, for by now another man, much more to Clarice's liking, had been appointed in his place.

If he is to remain permanently, Poliziano wrote desperately to Madonna Lucrezia, *then, indeed, I can assume that the bubble has burst. But I cannot believe it and, therefore, I beg you to find out what are Lorenzo's intentions, then I shall know whether to arm myself only for a tournament or for war.*

Poliziano was young as yet in the arts of courtiership, and was apt to overplay his hand.

Yesterday, he wrote again to Lucrezia, *we were told that Lorenzo was in a somewhat low state. God alone knows how it made me suffer. I am, therefore sending over Mariotto* (the Medici's barber) *in order to hear how he is. I would have come myself, but I was not sure whether or not I would be intruding. If there is anything I can do…*

People died suddenly in fifteenth-century Florence, and it was all too painfully clear to Poliziano that if anything happened to Lorenzo, then it would not take Clarice and her friends very long to turn him out of the Medici Court. In some vague way he could feel himself slipping already: this protector, this new foster-father whom he had grown to love, was turning away from him. Messengers were kept trotting over to Lucrezia's place with anxious enquiries – how was Lorenzo? What was he doing? The answer was that Lorenzo was ill with gout and overwork, and now the war was pushing him towards the major crisis of his life.

Then, too, with the loss of his tutorship, Poliziano was running short of money. Following his success at Florence, his relatives had descended upon him in a body. He put some of them up in rooms in the Via Fossi, near his Priory of San Paulo, and at Fiesole he took in his sister Maria and her family and a certain Tommaso, much given to tavern brawls. With this large household to support, he began manoeuvring for another church benefice; this was a living at Fiesole, in the gift of the Medicis.

I realise, he wrote to Lucrezia, *that this is not the moment to ask for anything – first on account of the thunderstorm* (the row with Clarice) *and then I might be told I have too much already. But the fact is, if I ever needed assistance, it is now. Besides being constantly drained by this sister of mine, the hopes I built on Piero are failing me.* The benefice, he adds reflectively, has quite a nice little estate attached to it.

But this time Lucrezia could not help him and the living went to someone else.

Yet, for the rest, it was a profitable summer; he translated the maxims of the Stoic philosopher Epictetus and Plutarch's *Amatoriae narrationes*, in addition to composing some of his best descriptive poems in Latin. Moreover, he began to settle into the work that became the ruling passion of his life – the collection, collation and translation of manuscripts for the Medici Library and the study of old coins and inscriptions. He was just 25 and his reputation as a scholar and a poet was now spreading all over Italy.

Up at Fiesole he worked in the Medici Platonic academy in the Badia Fiesolana. The church with its lovely Romanesque facade still remains along with some of the most graceful cloisters in Tuscany that lead off into the monastery. The place has been turned into a school now, and the upper rooms have been converted into dormitories for the boys, but you can still see the rooms where the library was kept before it was removed to Florence, and where Lorenzo, Poliziano, Ficino, Pico della Mirandola and probably Michelangelo, used to discuss philosophy through the night.

No doubt Poliziano might have continued happily at Fiesole, but in September 1479 the Florentines were overtaken by a major disaster in the war – their headquarters at Poggibonsi, near Siena, were overrun by the Papal and Neapolitan troops. Lorenzo's soldiers managed to struggle on into the winter, but it was obvious that when the enemy renewed their offensive in the spring, Florence itself must fall. Lorenzo made his famous decision to go to Naples and try to negotiate peace there with the King. It was a decision that needed something more than ordinary sangfroid, since the last envoy who had arrived at the King's Court had been immediately murdered. Moreover, it was upon Lorenzo himself – 'that ungrateful, excommunicated and heretical Lorenzo de' Medici' – that the Pope had sworn to take vengeance. Only a small party of Lorenzo's closest companions was to go on this dangerous mission.

On 4 December, Poliziano got wind that something was happening and that he was being kept out of it. He went to see his old friend, Madonna Lucrezia, and told her that he wanted to go with Lorenzo, whatever his plans might be. Lucrezia promised to pass this on to the Palazzo Medici. The rumour in Florence on that day was that Lorenzo was going to see the Pope, his principal enemy.

On 5 December, however, Poliziano heard that Lorenzo was not bound for Rome, but for Naples. But he had still not been asked to join the expedition, and so he went back to Lucrezia and repeated his eagerness to go. Then at last, early on the following morning, he was summoned by one of Lorenzo's secretaries, a man named Francesco, and told that he should be ready to leave at a moment's notice. When he asked where they were going, he was told Pisa. This he knew to be untrue; but when he tried to press the matter he got nothing but evasive answers.

This was the point where Poliziano began to make a fuss. He protested that he was being kept in the dark. Why was he being treated as an outsider like this? Were they going to Naples or not? And when? And for how long? He finished by saying that he would never enter into any engagement until he had talked to Lorenzo himself. And he went off to the Palazzo Medici and posted himself outside Lorenzo's door.

There he waited for an hour and a half without being summoned, not daring to go inside Lorenzo's room without an invitation. That hour and a half was probably the emotional crisis of Poliziano's life. It was one of those moments when one is assailed with dark misgivings about petty things – when there is no real guide to tell one how to act – and yet one feels that the chance of a lifetime may be slipping away. No doubt he was appalled by the dangers of the journey to Naples, but it was worse still that Lorenzo should go without him. Going or staying – they were both intolerable propositions.

It was not much good trying to rationalise the situation by saying that, after all, he was a poet, not a soldier or a politician, and he could not be expected to go; Lorenzo had asked for him and if he refused life in Florence would be impossible. It is not hard to imagine how, as he stood there outside the door, trying to catch attention, his mood of offended dignity began to subside into a welter of doubts and hesitations. Perhaps it was already too late: perhaps he had protested too much and Lorenzo had angrily struck him off the list.

Finally, when he could bear it no longer, he rushed off to see Francesco, and announced that he had changed his mind: he no longer wanted to talk to Lorenzo. He would go without asking more questions.

Leaving Francesco, he went off and got himself a coat for the journey; and then, much agitated, he returned to the Palazzo Medici again. The place was in an uproar. Tailors and embroiderers had been working through the night on Lorenzo's ambassadorial robes. Messengers kept flying in and out and Lorenzo remained closeted with his advisers. This time, however, Poliziano did succeed in getting admitted to his patron and actually had dinner with him. But Lorenzo remained deep in urgent conversation with other people.

Through the long afternoon Poliziano waited anxiously, growing more and more suspicious. One can picture him edging as close as he could to Lorenzo, talking – volubly no doubt – to anyone who looked as though he had any information, but never quite succeeding in drawing Lorenzo to one side.

By evening nobody yet had called him or given him any instructions and Poliziano was appalled to see Lorenzo set off for the Palazzo Vecchio, where forty members of the government had been gathered in secret session to hear his plans. The expedition was to leave Florence immediately after the meeting. In desperation Poliziano ran after Lorenzo, and was about to tug him by the sleeve, when Francesco called him back and told him that, on Lorenzo's orders, he was not to go. His place had been taken by someone else.

Poliziano says he was bewildered and hurt at this news. He hurried home and composed a letter, a last appeal, and this was sent in to Lorenzo, who was then in conference at the Palazzo Vecchio. It is doubtful if Lorenzo ever read the letter or even received it, for now he was entirely engulfed in his big adventure. He was making the speech, which he later confirmed in a letter, and which brought all his hearers to tears: 'Seeing that all other endeavours have been fruitless, I have determined to run some peril in my own person, rather than expose the city to disaster. Therefore, with the permission of Your Excellencies of the Signoria, I have decided to go openly to Naples. Being the one most hated and persecuted by our enemies, I may, by placing myself in their hands, be the means of restoring peace to our city... These are the feelings with which I go for perhaps our Lord God desires that this war, which began with the blood of my brother and my own, should be put an end to by me.'

Late that night Lorenzo left the city for the coast. A week later he set sail by galley for Naples. Utterly deflated, Poliziano roamed about Florence asking himself: 'Where shall I go? What shall I do?' For six years or more he had been the favourite in the Palazzo Medici; everybody had run after Angelo, asking him for favours, telling him how clever he was, and begging him to mention their names to Lorenzo. Now he had been publicly slighted by Lorenzo, and all Florence knew it about. And now, at last, Clarice had her revenge.

There is no record of what Clarice did the day after Lorenzo had gone. Possibly she did nothing, but simply let events take their course. However, the story quickly went around Florence that the favourite had been deposed: he had refused point blank to go to Naples. He had acted like a coward at a moment when the whole city was in danger and Lorenzo was risking his own life.

Technically, Poliziano was still in the pay of the Medici, and he was not at liberty to make any move without permission. No doubt the sensible thing for him to have done was to have gone quietly back to his books at Fiesole and waited there, well out of Clarice's way, until he saw what happened to Lorenzo in Naples. But he was unnerved. He did the foolish and precipitate thing: he quietly packed his clothes and left the city for Bologna in the north, a safe and neutral place.

To those who stayed behind in Florence, and to Lorenzo himself, now fighting for the freedom of the city of Naples, it seemed like the action of a traitor.

III

After he left Florence in 1479, Poliziano spent nearly eight months wandering in the Lombard cities of northern Italy. He drifted through Bologna, Mantua, Verona, Padua and Venice, picking up rich patrons where he could, browsing in libraries and talking to other scholars.

None of this brought him much peace of mind, for he soon realised that he had made a frightful mistake in abandoning Florence and Lorenzo. On 15 March 1480, Lorenzo arrived back from Naples with the news that the war against the Pope was over and Florence was saved. Poliziano lost no time in getting off a couple of complimentary poems to his old patron, together with a strong suggestion that he should be invited back to Florence again. He followed this with a long apologetic letter to Lorenzo, explaining just why he had deserted Florence, and asking for forgiveness. There was no reply either to the poems or the apology. Indeed, a fellow poet, Baccio Ugolini, who took Poliziano's letter down to Florence, reported back to him that he was much out of favour, and it was useless for him to try and return. Lorenzo regarded him as disloyal.

For the time being, then, Poliziano accepted exile. He got an appointment as house chaplain in the Court of Cardinal Gonzaga, at Mantua, and amused himself by writing a play, which he called *Orpheus*.

Orpheus is not perhaps one of the triumphs of Italian literature but it is a point of new departure in the art of the theatre. Up to this time the only plays shown in Italy were of a religious kind and mostly pantomime and spectacle. Three-decker stages were erected in the public squares – the upper part representing Paradise, the lower Hell, and the Earth lay in between. Devils in hideous masks were apt to come bursting up from Hell below, and angels chanted from Heaven above, while the main action took place on the central stage. There were elaborate contraptions for raising and lowering the actors through the air, and Brunelleschi is credited with once having designed an immense golden ball, out of which the Angel Gabriel sprang at the climax of the show. Usually performances opened with an improving discourse from the saints and angels, followed by a dance; and then one of the biblical parables was acted in dumb show. Garlands and tapestries were hung about, there were songs accompanied by the lute, and the whole thing made a very pretty spectacle against the background of the ancient buildings.

The point about *Orpheus* is that it was the first straight play to appear with a non-religious theme in the Italian language. You might even argue that it was the forerunner of Italian opera.

'I wrote this play,' Poliziano said later, 'at the request of the Most Reverend the Cardinal of Mantua, in the space of two days, among continual disturbances and in the vulgar tongue that it might be the better understood by the spectators.'

There seems to be no reason to doubt this. The original version of *Orpheus* consists of barely 400 lines, and it has the simplicity and gusto of a piece composed upon a single inspiration. Years afterwards, Poliziano affected to deplore its publication. 'Let it come out then,' he wrote rather archly to the printer, 'since such is your pleasure; but I suggest your kindness is a cruelty to me.' It is an imperfect child, he goes on, and he would have preferred to expose it, as the Spartans exposed their imperfect children on the hillsides, to destruction.

Even so, *Orpheus* is a *tour de force*, and has since been printed and played innumerable times. The story is simple, the fable of Orpheus and Eurydice, written in lyrical verse. It has, however, a slightly baffling ending: just at the tragic point where Orpheus turns round and Eurydice is snatched back to Hell, the action suddenly switches from pathos into bathos, and from bathos into a riot. In his rage and disappointment Orpheus declares he will never again love a woman, but instead, indulge himself with 'other (or new) flowers.' Bacchantes then rush upon the stage and tear Orpheus to pieces. The play ends with the bacchantes singing an exultant blood-song, followed by a drunken and orgiastic chant to Bacchus.

To some students that reference to 'other flowers' can mean only one thing – homosexuality (of which Poliziano is supposed to have been a leading exponent) – and there is some surprise that such a speech should have been made before a Cardinal. But this was the age of Pope Sixtus IV and the Borgias – indeed the play is dedicated to the future husband of Vanossa, the girl who became the mistress of Pope Alexander VI and the mother, by him, of Cesare and Lucrezia Borgia. A society which knew incest and a fathomless debauchery in Rome might have been pained but hardly surprised by a reference to homosexuality in a lyric poem.

Orpheus had an immediate success. It responded, like all of Poliziano's popular writings, to something in the age itself: that feeling men had then that they were living in a violent and barbarous time, a contemporary Hades, which could only be subdued by the Orpheus touch – by music and beauty and enlightenment.

But the poet was still yearning for Florence and Lorenzo. All through these months he kept up a barrage of epigrams and verses – 'I am yours, O Medici... I am yours for ever... Give back to me, my Lorenzo, your eyes, give back to me my happiness.' At last, in August, 1840, Lorenzo called him back. Possibly the success of *Orpheus* had something to do with it.

When Lorenzo forgave he forgave handsomely. He reinstated Poliziano as tutor to his eldest son, Piero, and even appointed him professor of Latin and Greek eloquence at the Studio Florentino.

Poliziano was a tremendous speaker. It is said that he made no great impression when he first came into the lecture room, with that squinting eye and the huge hooked nose. But when he began to speak he charmed everyone who heard him, and they would sit spell-bound until he finished. Some of the ablest scholars of Europe journeyed to Florence to hear him and even his old professors came and sat as pupils at his feet. He discoursed upon nearly all the classical authors, explaining and commenting upon the text with a staggering memory. To anyone who is not passionately interested in squeezing out fine shades of meaning from a diphthong or an unaccented vowel, these commentaries make pretty heavy going when they are read now. But at that time, when rhetoric was the fashion, these things were fascinating.

Poliziano spoke for two hours in the morning and two hours in the afternoon, alternating Greek and Latin. He had a trick of introducing his subject through some very simple and homely idea, and so you get some pretty surprising things scattered through his lectures. 'They say,' he once began, 'that the female mouse is madly lustful.'

At night he often walked or rode with Lorenzo and discussed with him all the matters that had been raised in the lecture-room through the day. It was Lorenzo who had first persuaded Poliziano to write in Italian and they still composed songs and jingles together. But now, at the age of 26, Poliziano was turning back to the classics again, and the popular poet was rapidly becoming lost in the professor. Under his charge the Florentine library was becoming the most distinguished in Europe. At this time, Lorenzo had agents all over the less barbarous parts of the Continent, and in the Near East, searching for classical manuscripts, and he paid large prices for them. The pearl of his collection was the *Pandects of Justinian*, which was kept under armed guard in the vaults of the Palazzo Vecchio. Since the manuscript was too precious to be moved, Poliziano studied it there, in the light of torches.

Meanwhile, Poliziano's reputation was overflowing. He wrote to his friend Hieronymous Donatus: 'If anyone wants a motto for the hilt of his sword, a phrase for a ring, an inscription for his bedroom or a device for his plate or even his pots and pans, he runs like everybody else to Poliziano. There is hardly a wall I have not besmeared like a snail with the effusions of my brain. One man pesters me for rhymes and drinking songs, another for a grave discourse, a third for a serenade and a fourth for a licentious carnival ballad. This fool tells me his love troubles, which I sit like a fool to hear. Another asks me for a symbol which will baffle the curiosity of the others and which only his mistress will understand. I pass over the unreasonable garrulity of the pedants, the impertinences of the poetasters who are constantly admiring their own productions. These are the plagues I am compelled to endure every day, beside the interruptions I meet with in my walks from the lower classes of this city and its vicinity – they drag me through the streets like an ox through the nose.'

Financially things were going very well indeed with him: he still had his church benefices, to which he added a few more and, in 1483, Lorenzo gave him the Villa Diana, near the little hamlet of Fontelucente (which means 'shining fountain') on the steep north-western side of Fiesole. Here he spent the hot summer months during the remainder of his life and composed his *Sylvae*, one of the most famous of his works. It is a long Latin poem, divided into four books, and is intended to be an introduction to poetry from the time of Hesiod to Dante.

Lorenzo had a habit of bestowing Fiesole villas on his followers and there were now quite a few of them scattered over the hillside. The most notable of these was Poliziano's closest friend, Pico della Mirandola. It was said that a ball of fire appeared in the sky over his mother's bed-chamber when Pico was born; it burnt itself out quickly. Pico was nine years younger than Poliziano, and he died within a month or two of Poliziano at the age of 32. The fire that burned in Pico in those few years was incredible. He was credited with speaking 22 languages, he was a poet and a prince, and his vast learning was said to cover all the known philosophies of the East. Pico was one of the first and most distinguished scholars to abandon the luxuries of Renaissance Italy and join Savonarola's crusade for poverty and repentance.

There is a charming description of this conversion by Sir Thomas More, who first introduced Pico to England. 'Before this,' he says, 'Pico had been both desirous of glory and kindled in vain love, and holden in voluptuous use of women. The comeliness of his body, with the lovely favour of his visage, and therewithal his marvellous frame, his excellent learning, great richness and noble kindred, set many women afire on him. From the desire of whom he not abhorring was somewhat fallen into wantonness. But... he drew back his mind flowing in riot, and turned it to Christ.'

In an unexplained footnote to his manuscript. Sir Thomas added pleasantly: 'The best of us all hath had a madding time.'

It was mostly with Pico and Lorenzo, and one or two others, that Poliziano used to sit up dreaming, and arguing through the night in a gentle glow of Platonic philosophy, worlds upon worlds opening out before them. The talk was endless. They used to keep a light burning before a bust of Plato and every year there was a banquet to celebrate the great man's birthday. Voltaire goes so far as to suggest that these men were 'superior perhaps to the boasted sages of Greece', which seems extravagant. Yet they did feel that they were on the edge of tremendous things, as in fact they were. Underneath all the heavy-handed rhetoric there is a continuous sense of excitement and discovery, since it was not only the future that was opening up but the past as well.

Every day something new happened and Poliziano's life was a wonderful mixture of the naif and the sublime. On Monday he is agog over the discovery of four lost books of Cicero and on Tuesday he is marvelling over the arrival of a giraffe, the gift of the Sultan of Egypt to Lorenzo. He dismisses the discovery of printing with the words: 'The most stupid ideas can now in a moment be transferred into a thousand volumes and spread abroad,' but he is much intrigued by the report that a nest of witches has been found at Fiesole, behind the Villa Diana. Pier Leone, Lorenzo's doctor, announces that he has discovered a wonderful new remedy made of the oil of scorpions and the tongues of asps; and Toscanelli, the geographer, produces a chart which pretends that the world might not, after all, be flat. He has been corresponding about it with a Florentine merchant named Amerigo Vespucci and a young Genovese called Christopher Columbus.

All these things were jumbled up in Poliziano's mind, together with the most advanced scholarship, and a remarkable facility in composing Latin verse. When Michelangelo turned up at the age of 16, he was quickly gathered into the Fiesolean circle. Poliziano met him in the Garden of Clarice, the sculptor's school which Lorenzo had established just off the Piazza San Marco, and was enraptured with him. One of the best of Michelangelo's early works, the bas-relief of the battle of the centaurs, was suggested to him by Poliziano.

Through all these years Poliziano worked prodigiously. When he went down to Rome, in 1484, with his pupil Piero de' Medici, he took with him his translation of Herodian, to present to the Pope. He said he had finished it in two days, walking up and down his room dictating to secretaries. The Pope gave him 200 gold crowns for the manuscript, which has since found its way back to the Laurentian Library in Florence. It does indeed appear to have been written down by several copyists and Poliziano has gone over the sheets with his neat handwriting, correcting the work and signing his name at the end.

One has this same impression of haste about most of Poliziano's friends: it is as though they sensed that they had very little time before some terrible and inevitable disaster came bearing down on them and put a stop to all their discoveries. They had the feeling, too, that in the midst of all this exploration, they were losing touch with the ordinary patterns and morals of life. Where were they heading to and what did it all mean? Who was going to control what they created? It was a feeling, in fact, that has a certain familiar ring in the fifties.

Meanwhile Lorenzo's family was growing up. Piero, the eldest boy, was now aged 17, and in 1488 Poliziano again went down to Rome with him for his marriage to Alfonsina Orsini. Lorenzo's wife, Clarice, Poliziano's old enemy, felt very ill at the wedding, and a few weeks later she returned to Florence to die. She was only 37.

But Poliziano went triumphantly onward. Now he had Lorenzo to himself, and he even began corresponding on fairly intimate terms with other rulers in Europe. 'By the kindness and liberality of Lorenzo de' Medici,' he wrote to the King of Hungary, 'I have been raised from an obscure birth and humble fortune to the degree of rank and distinction I now enjoy. I have, for a series of years, publicly taught at Florence, not only the Latin language with universal applause, but likewise Greek, which I venture to affirm has been the case with no other Italian for a thousand years past.'

In the same unabashed strain, he wrote to the King of Portugal suggesting he should become the King's historian, lest his doings should 'lie hidden in the vast heap of human frailty.' Only through the minds of learned men, Poliziano said, could kings hope for immortality. The King of Portugal was inclined to agree with him and actually sent off some material for Poliziano to work on; but by then (1492) it was already too late. Lorenzo was dying, Savonarola was looming over Florence, crying 'Repentance: the deluge is coming,' and presently Poliziano himself was swept away.

Poliziano was almost the last of Lorenzo's followers to go over to Savonarola. When Pico was converted to austerity, along with Botticelli, Fra Bartolommeo and nearly all the other artists, he still hung back, for it was impossible for him to imagine life without Lorenzo. He saw, perhaps, more clearly than the others, that Savonarola was the real enemy of Lorenzo: his movement meant the end of everything Lorenzo and Poliziano believed in – man's free will, to be elegant, to win fame, to accept good and evil as inevitable in human life, and to have the right, if you chose, to worship Plato as well as Christ.

Life, for Poliziano, was here and now and it was a wonderful thing – not, as this gloomy friar suggested, a brief and sinful interlude, to be got through in the most dismal possible way.

But, in the early spring of 1492, Lorenzo's gout grew worse, and he was in constant pain. On 10 March, after immense contriving, his second son Giovanni was made a Cardinal; but Lorenzo himself had to be carried on a litter into the banquet of celebration in the Medici Palace, and he ate nothing. When Giovanni went off to Rome a few days later Lorenzo collapsed. On 21 March he was taken out to his villa at Careggi, where his father and his grandfather had died before him.

Poliziano was at Careggi when Lorenzo died, and his account of how it happened is probably the authentic one.

'The day before his death,' he says, 'being at Careggi, he grew so weak that all hope of his recovery vanished. Perceiving this, like a wise man, he called for the confessor to purge himself of past sins... Rousing himself, he exclaimed, "It shall never be said that my Lord, who created and saved me, shall come to me – in my room – raise me, I beg you, raise me quickly, so that I may go and meet Him." Saying this, he raised himself as well as he could and, supported by his servants, advanced to meet the priest in the outer room. There, crying, he knelt down... At length the priest ordered that he should be raised from the ground and carried to his bed, so that he could receive the Viaticum in more comfort. For some time he resisted, but at last, out of respect for the priest, he consented. In bed, repeating almost the same prayer as he had before, with much gravity and devotion, he received the body and blood of Christ.'

The doctor then arrived. 'He seemed most learned,' Poliziano says, 'but was summoned too late to be of any use. Yet, to do something, he ordered various precious stones to be pounded together in a mortar, for I know not what kind of medicine. Lorenzo, thereupon asked the servants what the doctor was doing in his room, and what he was preparing, and when I answered that he was composing a remedy to comfort his intestines, he recognised my voice, and looking kindly, as he used to do, he said: "Oh, Angiolo, are you here?" and, raising his languid arms took both my hands and pressed them tightly. I could not stifle my sobs or hold back my tears, though I tried to hide them by turning my face away. But he showed no emotion and continued to press my hands between his. When he saw I could not speak for crying quite naturally he loosened my hands and I ran into the adjoining room.'

Then Pico arrived and finally Savonarola, who gave Lorenzo his Benediction. 'Bowing his head, immersed in piety and religion, he repeated the words and the prayers of the friar, without paying any attention to the grief now shown openly by his attendants. It seemed that all save Lorenzo were going to die, so calm he was. He gave no signs of anxiety or sorrow: even in that supreme moment he showed his usual strength of mind and his fortitude. The doctors who stood round, not to seem idle, worried him with their remedies and assistance. He submitted to everything they suggested, not because he thought it would save him, but in order not to offend anyone, even in death.

To the last he had such mastery over himself that he joked about his own death. Thus, when given something to eat and asked how he liked it he replied: 'As well as a dying man can like anything.' He embraced us all tenderly and humbly asked pardon if, during his illness, he had caused annoyance to anyone. Then, disposing himself to receive extreme unction, he commended his soul to God.'

Poliziano's life flew to bits. He did not go so far as the doctor, Pier Leone, who, having been terrified of drowning all his life (he once refused to take a job in Venice on account of the canals) committed suicide in a well. But he crept about Florence and Fiesole uttering laments: 'Oh that my head were waters and mine eyes a fountain of tears, that I might weep day and night. So mourns the turtle dove, so mourns the dying swan, so mourns the nightingale. Lightning has struck our laurel tree, beneath whose spreading boughs the god of song himself more sweetly harped and sang. Now all around is dumb, now all is mute and there are none to hear.'

Poliziano hung on for another two years, but he accomplished nothing. There is a feeble moth-like quality about his movements: he still fluttered about Florence and Fiesole, but with a bewildered air as though he could not understand where all the warmth and happiness had gone. He seems to have been surrounded by enemies at the end, for he was known to everyone as Lorenzo's man: and the reaction against Lorenzo was violent. His old pupil Piero, now the head of the State, tried to get him a Cardinal's hat but that fell through; and Piero, himself, on whom Poliziano had poured out all his genius as a teacher, was turning out to be a disastrous failure.

Even the silly business over Alessandra Scala went wrong. Alessandra was a notable blue-stocking in Florence, a poetress and a scholar, and there had been a time when Poliziano imagined he was in love with her. He reached the stage of sending little gifts and exchanging Greek epigrams with her. But Alessandra abruptly broke this off and married, instead, the Greek scholar Marullus, who from a friend had become one of Poliziano's worst enemies. This led to a bitter and abusive quarrel – one of a number of quarrels that bedevilled these last days of his life.

One after another most of his friends vanished – either they died or they crept to Savonarola for repentance. In Florence now there was an almost hysterical reaction towards austerity: it was an emotional excitement for people to make huge public bonfires of their wigs and extravagant carnival clothes. They gathered trembling from early morning at the cathedral to hear Savonarola and feel their flesh creep as he thundered out his terrible prophecies. But for Poliziano it was meaningless: for him life was over anyway. The best of it evaporated at Lorenzo's death. If there existed a God, then he was some radiant Platonic figure, a benign intellectual, the universal Patron, who was infinitely tolerant and kind.

To Poliziano, Lorenzo's Florence had been heaven, and this monastic, silent, apprehensive city was hell. He wanted no part of it. It had been a wonderful interlude while Lorenzo was alive and now he was the guest who had stayed too long.

Poliziano lived just long enough to see the beginnings of the destruction of everything he had loved and worked for – the looting of the Palazzo Medici and the dispersal of the books in the library, the expulsion of Piero de' Medici, the decline and death of his friends, and the overwhelming of Italy itself by the barbarians coming down from the north. To Poliziano, all this – and he had a glimpse of it before he died – meant nothing less than the return of the dark ages. They had escaped from violence and barbarity for a little – he and Lorenzo and the others. Now they were being sucked back into the darkness again. Poliziano was not a very strong character. He gave up at last. He went down to Savonarola's Church of San Marco and begged to be buried there when he died. His last illness coincides very neatly with the end of the era.

There was one last rather wistful letter written to his old master Ficino, from the Villa Diana:

I hope when your Careggi becomes too hot in August you will not spurn this little Fiesolan country place of ours. Here we have many springs, and since we are in a narrow valley, there is a little sun; certainly we are never without a breeze. The little villa lies hidden away from the road and almost in the middle of a wood, yet even so it has a view over all Florence, and although there are a great many people hereabouts, yet there is always that solitude which the contemplative love. You will also be able to have a two-fold pleasure here, for often stealing unannounced from his oak-grove Pico visits me and, having dragged me from my hiding place, takes me with him to dinner which I have indeed known to be frugal but always both sensible and full of delightful conversation and amusement. Nevertheless you had better stay with me because you will not eat worse here and perhaps you will drink better, since in the matter of wines I would be a strong rival even of Pico. Vale.

Angelo Poliziano

After that he left the Villa and went down to Florence.

There are several versions of his actual death – most of them rather unsavoury. 'Poliziano, that fine genius who spoke Latin so well, was called Angelo,' runs the most popular account, 'but he was far from possessing the purity of one of the angelic choir. The abominable passion he entertained for a youth, Greek by birth, occasioned his death, and has forever dishonoured his memory. For in a paroxysm of amorous fever, he suddenly got up one night while his attendant was asleep, and taking his lute in his hand, went to play and sing under the young Greek's window. He was fetched home half dead, and being put to bed, expired shortly afterwards.'

A second version states that he died 'from knocking his head against the wall in a fury of amorous impatience of the most disgraceful character.' Still another version runs – 'He was singing on the staircase some verses he had composed for a former mistress of his (Alessandra ?), when he came to a very tender passage, his lute fell from his hand, and he tumbled head foremost downstairs and broke his neck.'

On investigation, there seems not to be a word of truth in any of this; and it is highly probable that the story was put about by Marullus in the first place.

What actually happened, so far as one can judge, was that Poliziano became converted to Savonarola shortly before he died. He had rooms in the Garden of Clarice, just across the street from Savonarola's Church of San Marco, and he used to teach the monks there. One of the monks, Roberto Ubaldini, records that he was often with Poliziano during his last illness and was at his bedside in his rooms when he died. At Poliziano's own request he was received into the Domenican Order just before the end, and he was buried in the habit of a monk. The coffin was placed in the laymen's cemetery by the wall of the church; and a few weeks later he was joined there by Pico. That marvellous beauty of Pico and his radiant reputation stayed with him to the end.

Up at the Villa Diana not much remains to remind you of Poliziano. We have ghosts, of course, but amiable ones. I personally have never seen anything, but our guests are constantly saying when they come down to breakfast in the morning that they have suddenly woken in the night and heard voices all around them; not menacing or frightening voices, rather pleasant ones, as though a group of friends were having a cheerful conversation. But when the guests put the light on they see nothing. There's another, more prosaic form of haunting too; on a still summer night a cool breeze suddenly comes spiriting through the house and this I *can* vouch for. But whether or not it is due to psychic influence or simply the draught coming through an open window I cannot say.

Down in San Marco in Florence they put up a facetious epitaph after Poliziano's death. It read: 'Poliziano lies in this grave, the angel who had one head and, what is new, three tongues. He died September 24, 1494, aged forty.'

Later on the monks felt that this was hardly adequate for the greatest poet-scholar of the Renaissance. The epitaph, which was engraved on a small rectangular stone, was relegated to a back room and the coffin shifted to a better place. To-day the eager tourist will find that a fine white marble tablet has been let into the wall in the nave just below Pico's tomb. It reads:

Here lie the re-discovered bones of Angelo Ambrogini called Poliziano, 1454–1494, the master and poet of the three most divine languages of Europe, who wanted the Athens of Pericles to rise again in the Florence of the Magnificent.

In 1939 both Pico's and Poliziano's graves were opened. By some chemistry of the elements, as though they wished to confirm the popular reputation of the two men, the body of Pico was found to be excellently preserved. Poliziano, however, had crumbled into bones and dust.

For a time these remains were stowed in a drawer in the sacristy and the old prior of San Marco would show them to visitors there. There was nothing much to evoke the poet in that grey decay. After one curious glance the visitors would turn away and the prior closed the drawer again.

www.summersdale.com